The Basics of Information Security

The Basics of Information Security

Understanding the Fundamentals of InfoSec in Theory and Practice

Jason Andress

Technical Editor
Russ Rogers

Amsterdam • Boston • Heidelberg • London • New York
Oxford • Paris • San Diego • San Francisco
Singapore • Sydney • Tokyo

Syngress Press is an imprint of Elsevier

Acquiring Editor: Angelina Ward
Development Editor: Heather Scherer
Project Manager: Jessica Vaughan
Designer: Alisa Andreola

Syngress is an imprint of Elsevier
225 Wyman Street, Waltham, MA 02451, USA

Notices

Knowledge and best practice in this field are constantly changing. As new research and experience broaden our understanding, changes in research methods or professional practices, may become necessary. Practitioners and researchers must always rely on their own experience and knowledge in evaluating and using any information or methods described herein. In using such information or methods they should be mindful of their own safety and the safety of others, including parties for whom they have a professional responsibility.

To the fullest extent of the law, neither the Publisher nor the authors, contributors, or editors, assume any liability for any injury and/or damage to persons or property as a matter of products liability, negligence or otherwise, or from any use or operation of any methods, products, instructions, or ideas contained in the material herein.

Library of Congress Cataloging-in-Publication Data
Andress, Jason.
  The basics of information security : understanding the fundamentals of InfoSec in theory and practice/ Jason Andress.
    p. cm.
  Includes index.
  ISBN 978-1-59749-653-7
  1. Computer security. 2. Computer networks–Security measures. 3. Information resources management.
I. Title.
  QA76.9.A25A5453 2011
  005.8–dc23   2011013969

British Library Cataloguing-in-Publication Data
A catalogue record for this book is available from the British Library.

ISBN: 978-1-59749-653-7

11 12 13 14 15 10 9 8 7 6 5 4 3 2 1
Printed in the United States of America

For information on all Syngress publications visit our website at www.syngress.com

Dedication

Many thanks go to my family for persevering through another project. Additionally, thanks to Russ for a great job tech editing, and to Steve Winterfeld for being willing to jump in and help. Steve, you're a fine acquisitions editor, and you don't get nearly the credit that you should.

Contents

Jason Andress (ISSAP, CISSP, GPEN, CEH) is a seasoned security professional with a depth of experience in both the academic and business worlds. He is presently employed by a major software company, providing global information security oversight, and performing penetration testing, risk assessment, and compliance functions to ensure that the company's assets are protected.

Jason has taught undergraduate and graduate security courses since 2005 and holds a doctorate in computer science, researching in the area of data protection. He has authored several publications and books, writing on topics including data security, network security, penetration testing, and digital forensics.

About the Technical Editor

Russ Rogers (CISSP, CISM, IAM, IEM, HonScD), author of the popular *Hacking a Terror Network* (Syngress, ISBN 1-928994-98-9); coauthor of multiple other books including the best-selling *Stealing the Network: How to Own a Continent* (Syngress, ISBN 1-931836-05-1), *Network Security Evaluation Using the NSA IEM* (Syngress, 1-597490-35-0), and former editor-in-chief of *The Security Journal*; is currently a penetration tester for a federal agency and the cofounder and chief executive officer of Peak Security, Inc., a veteran-owned small business based in Colorado Springs, CO. He has been involved in information technology since 1980 and has spent the last 20 years working professionally as both an IT and INFOSEC consultant. He has worked with the United States Air Force (USAF), National Security Agency (NSA), Defense Information Systems Agency (DISA), and other federal agencies. He is a globally renowned security expert, speaker, and author who has presented at conferences around the world including Amsterdam, Tokyo, Singapore, Sao Paulo, Abu Dhabi, and cities all over the United States.

Russ has an honorary doctorate of science in information technology from the University of Advancing Technology, a master's degree in computer systems management from the University of Maryland, a bachelor of science in computer information systems from the University of Maryland, and an associate degree in applied communications technology from the Community College of the Air Force. He is currently pursuing a bachelor of science in electrical engineering from the University of Colorado at Colorado Springs. He is a member of ISSA and ISC2 (CISSP). He also teaches at and fills the role of professor of network security for the University of Advancing Technology (http://www.uat.edu).

Russ would like to thank his children, his father, and Tracie for being so supportive over the years. Thanks and shout-outs go out to Chris Hurley, Mark Carey, Rob Bathurst, Pushpin, Paul Criscuolo, Ping Look, Greg Miles, Ryan Clarke, Luke McOmie, Curtis Letson, and Eddie Mize.

Boring, boring, boring. Isn't this what immediately comes to mind when one sees books on foundational concepts of information security? Monotonous coverage of theory, dry details of history, brief yet inadequate coverage of every topic known to man, even though you know that you'll never be hired by the NSA as a cryptographer. All you really want is a book that makes you fall asleep every 30 minutes instead of every five. It's all the "necessary evil" that must be endured, right? Not this time, my budding security professional.

So let's be honest. You actually do have a strong interest in making security a career and not just a hobby. Why else would you have this book in your hand? But like many of you, I didn't know (and sometimes still wonder to this day) what I wanted to be when I grew up. So why this book? What's so great about another extensive volume on information security? How does it help me not only to learn the basics but also to push my career aspirations in the right direction?

When my son was 4, I took him to the park down the road from our house. There were kids playing baseball, others chasing their friends through the plastic and metal jungle, and even a few climbing the fake rock-climbing wall. Then he saw the boys at the skateboard park. He had a board of his own but never knew someone could do that! Of course, he wanted to try it immediately. As a responsible Dad, I couldn't let him launch himself off the top of a 6-foot ramp only to end up unconscious waiting to be run over by the next prepubescent wannabe Tony Hawk. But what I could do is require him to show me that he could do something basic like stand on the board and ride it all the way down the driveway at home. As a reward, he could go to the skate park. Once there, he didn't feel quite as comfortable as when on the driveway, so he rode down the ramp while sitting. Eventually, he dictated his own path; he set his own goals; he controlled the time it took to get where he wanted to be.

His path was different from many others at the park that day. But imagine if we never went to the park. How about if he only saw a baseball being tossed and no home runs? What if he didn't even get to see the skate park, much less the kids airing the gap? Knowing what is possible can drastically change one's destiny. And so it is with a profession in security.

Simply wanting a career in information security is not specific enough to convey all the possible job descriptions in an industry that now touches every other. What Dr. Andress has done, in addition to giving a solid foundation, is make your neurons spark. It's those sparks that have the "intended" consequence of giving career advice. How does he do this? Instead of just sticking to the tried and true classroom tactics of presenting the information and requiring rote memorization, he cleverly intermixes hacking, forensics, and many other sexy topics (that, again being completely honest, got most of us hot about getting into security in the first place), and shows us where it all fits in the grand scheme of the entire information security landscape. So instead of just covering the required topics, he avoids the boredom by giving glimpses of what the future could be for the reader such as in

- Chapter 3, Authorization and Access Control, where he discusses the confused deputy problem with real-world examples of CSRF and clickjacking.
- Chapter 4, Auditing and Accountability, with the coverage of vulnerability assessments and penetration testing and the difference between the two, an important concept not seen in many introductory security tomes.
- Chapter 5, Cryptography, with the suggestion of trying a DIY project by building your own Enigma machine to crack Germany's secret codes during World War II.
- Chapter 8, Network Security, and Chapter 9, Operating System Security, where the reader doesn't just read about the concepts but is shown actual screenshots of hacking tools such as Wireshark, Kismet, Nmap, and Metasploit to get the job done.

I wasn't sure why Jason asked me, the editor-in-chief of an online hacking magazine, to write the foreword to a security book that clearly is introductory in nature. Then, as I read the book and eventually shared the examples above, it became clear that Jason not only had a sincere desire to share his knowledge of information security, but he also wanted to impart the mindset of a hacker. In a word, a hacker is a tinkerer. A hacker is someone who just can't help himself from exploring and getting more out of the object of his attention, whether that be a car, a toaster, a computer, or a network. If you can grasp half of the mindset that Jason shows in this book, you'll be well on your way.

Inspiring, inspiring, inspiring. Each step along the way, Jason brilliantly peppers the foundational topics with gems of real-world applications. In doing so, he not only inspires the reader but also slyly helps you determine the path of your InfoSec career. Certain tidbits will grab your eye. Many examples will make you jot down a quick note to explore the topic further. There will even be times when you feel like you can't help but put the book down and research the hell out of what you just read. If Jason makes you do that at any point in this book, please take a moment to really process what it is that made your blood flow. It's a sure sign that this is a topic for which a career could be imminent. Don't take that lightly. I know if you were in a classroom with him, he wouldn't let you.

So what are you waiting for? Dive into this book, get the foundation you need, find the hacker mindset in yourself and discover where your passion lies.

Good luck!

Donald C. Donzal, CISSP, MCSE, Security + SME

Editor-in-Chief

The Ethical Hacker Network

Introduction

BOOK OVERVIEW AND KEY LEARNING POINTS

The *Basics of Information Security* will provide the reader with a basic knowledge of information security in both theoretical and practical aspects. We will first cover the basic knowledge needed to understand the key concepts of information security, discussing many of the concepts that underpin the security world. We will then dive into practical applications of these ideas in the areas of operations, physical, network, operating system, and application security.

BOOK AUDIENCE

This book will provide a valuable resource to beginning security professionals, as well as to network and systems administrators. The information provided in this book can be used to develop a better understanding of how we protect our information assets and defend against attacks, as well as how to apply these concepts practically.

Those in management positions will find this information useful as well, from the standpoint of developing better overall security practices for their organizations. The concepts discussed in this book can be used to drive security projects and policies, in order to mitigate some of the issues discussed.

HOW THIS BOOK IS ORGANIZED

This book is designed to take the reader through a logical progression for a foundational understanding of information security and is best read in the order of the chapters from front to back. In the areas where we refer to information located in other chapters in the book, we have endeavored to point out where the information can be found. The following descriptions will provide an overview of the contents of each chapter:

Chapter 1: What Is Information Security?

In this chapter, we cover some of the most basic concepts of information security. Information security is vital in the era in which data regarding countless individuals and organizations is stored in a variety of computer systems, often not under our direct control. We talk about the diametrically opposing concepts of security and productivity, the models that are helpful in discussing security concepts, such as the confidentiality, integrity, and availability (CIA) triad and the Parkerian hexad, as well as the basic concepts of risk and controls to mitigate it. Lastly, we cover defense in depth and its place in the information security world.

Chapter 2: Identification and Authentication

In Chapter 2, we cover the security principles of identification and authentication. We discuss identification as a process by which we assert the identity of a particular party, whether this is true or not. We talk about the use of authentication as the means of validating whether the claim of identity is true. We also cover multifactor authentication and the use of biometrics and hardware tokens to enhance surety in the authentication process.

Chapter 3: Authorization and Access Control

In this chapter, we discuss the use of authorization and access control. Authorization is the next step in the process that we work through in order to allow entities access to resources. We cover the various access control models that we use when putting together such systems like discretionary access control, mandatory access control, and role-based access control. We also talk about multilevel access control models, including Bell LaPadula, Biba, Clark-Wilson, and Brewer and Nash. In addition to the commonly discussed concepts of logical access control, we also go over some of the specialized applications that we might see when looking specifically at physical access control.

Chapter 4: Auditing and Accountability

We discuss the use of auditing and accountability in this chapter. We talk about the need to hold others accountable when we provide access to the resources on which our businesses are based, or to personal information of a sensitive nature. We also go over the processes that we carry out in order to ensure that our environment is compliant with the laws, regulations, and policies that bind it, referred to as auditing. In addition, we address the tools that we use to support audit, accountability, and monitoring activities, such as logging and monitoring.

Chapter 5: Cryptography

In this chapter, we discuss the use of cryptography. We go over the history of such tools, from very simple substitution ciphers to the fairly complex electro-mechanical machines that were used just before the invention of the first modern computing systems and how they form the basis for many of our modern algorithms. We cover the three main categories of cryptographic algorithms: symmetric key cryptography, also known as private key cryptography, asymmetric key cryptography, and hash functions. We also talk about digital signatures that can be used to ensure that data has not been altered and certificates that allow us to link a public key to a particular identity. In addition, we cover the mechanisms that we use to protect data at rest, in motion, and, to a certain extent, in use.

Chapter 6: Operations Security

This chapter covers operational security. We talk about the history of operational security, which reaches at least as far back as the writings of Sun Tzu in the sixth century BC to the words of George Washington, writings from the business community, and formal methodologies from the U.S. government. We talk about the five major steps of operations security: identifying critical information, analyzing threats, analyzing vulnerabilities, determining risks, and planning countermeasures. We also go over the Laws of OPSEC, as penned by Kurt Haas. In addition to discussing the use of operations security in the worlds of business and government, we also address how it is used in our personal lives, although perhaps in a less formal manner.

Chapter 7: Physical Security

In this chapter, we discuss physical security. We address the main categories of physical security controls, to include deterrent, detective, and preventive measures, and discuss how they might be put in place to mitigate physical security issues. We talk about the foremost concern in physical security, ensuring the safety of our people and talk about how data and equipment can generally be replaced, when proper precautions are taken, though people can be very difficult to replace. We also cover the protection of data, secondary only to protecting our people, and how this is a highly critical activity in our world of technology-based business. Lastly, we discuss protecting our equipment, both outside of and within our facilities.

Chapter 8: Network Security

In this chapter, we examine how we might protect our networks from a variety of different angles. We go over secure network design and segmentation properly, ensuring that we have the proper choke points to enable control of traffic, and that we are redundant where such is needed. We look into the implementation of security devices such as firewalls and intrusion detection systems, the protection of our network traffic with virtual private networks (VPNs) and security measures specific to wireless networks when we need to use them, and make use of secure protocols. We also consider a variety of security tools, such as Kismet, Wireshark, nmap, honeypots, and other similar utilities.

Chapter 9: Operating System Security

In this chapter, we explore hardening as one of the primary tools for securing the operating system and the steps that we take to do so. We also review the additional security-related software that we might use to secure our systems including anti-malware tools, software firewalls, and host-based intrusion detection systems in order to protect us from a variety of attacks. Lastly, we touch on some of the security tools that we can use from an operating perspective, including port scanners such as nmap, vulnerability analysis tools such as Nessus, and exploit frameworks such as Metasploit.

Chapter 10: Application Security

In this chapter, we consider the various ways in which we might secure our applications. We go over the vulnerabilities common to the software development process, including buffer overflows, race conditions, input validation attacks, authentication attacks, authorization attacks, and cryptographic attacks, and how we might mitigate these by following secure coding guidelines. We talk about Web security, the areas of concern on both the client-side issues and server side of the technology. We introduce database security and cover protocol issues, unauthenticated access, arbitrary code execution, and privilege escalation, and the measures that we might take to mitigate such issues. Lastly, we examine security tools from an application perspective, including sniffers such as Wireshark, fuzzing tools including some developed by Microsoft, and Web application analysis tools such as Burp Suite in order to better secure our applications.

CONCLUSION

Writing this book was an adventure for the author, as always. We hope that you enjoy the end result and that we expand your view into the world of information security. The security world can be an interesting and, at times, hair-raising field to work in. Welcome and good luck!

CHAPTER 1

What is Information Security?

Information in This Chapter:
- What is Security?
- Models for Discussing Security Issues
- Attacks
- Defense in Depth

INTRODUCTION

Information security is a concept that becomes ever more enmeshed in many aspects of our society, largely as a result of our nearly ubiquitous adoption of computing technology. In our everyday lives, many of us work with computers for our employers, play on computers at home, go to school online, buy goods from merchants on the Internet, take our laptops to the coffee shop and check our e-mail, carry our smartphones on our hips and use them to check our bank balances, track our exercise with sensors in our shoes, and so on, ad infinitum.

Although this technology enables us to be more productive and allows us to access a host of information with only a click of the mouse, it also carries with it a host of security issues. If the information on the systems used by our employers or our banks becomes exposed to an attacker, the consequences can be dire indeed. We could suddenly find ourselves bereft of funds, as the contents of our bank account are transferred to a bank in another country in the middle of the night. Our employer could lose millions of dollars, face legal prosecution, and suffer damage to its reputation because of a system configuration issue allowing an attacker to gain access to a database containing personally identifiable information (PII) or proprietary information. We see such issues appear in the media with disturbing regularity.

If we look back 30 years, such issues related to computer systems were nearly nonexistent, largely due to the low level of technology and the few people who were using what was in place. Although technology changes at an increasingly rapid rate, and specific implementations arise on a seemingly daily basis, much of the theory that discusses how we go about keeping ourselves secure changes at a much slower pace and does not always keep up with the changes to our technology. If we can gain a good understanding of the basics of information security, we are on a strong footing to cope with changes as they come along.

WHAT IS SECURITY?

Information security is defined as *"protecting information and information systems from unauthorized access, use, disclosure, disruption, modification, or destruction,"* according to U.S. law [1]. In essence, it means we want to protect our data and our systems from those who would seek to misuse it.

In a general sense, security means protecting our assets. This may mean protecting them from attackers invading our networks, natural disasters, adverse environmental conditions, power failures, theft or vandalism, or other undesirable states. Ultimately, we will attempt to secure ourselves against the most likely forms of attack, to the best extent we reasonably can, given our environment.

When we look at what exactly it is that we secure, we may have a broad range of potential assets. We can consider physical items that we might want to secure, such as those of inherent value (e.g., gold bullion) or those that have value to our business (e.g., computing hardware). We may also have items of a more ethereal nature, such as software, source code, or data. In today's computing environment, we are likely to find that our logical assets are at least as valuable as, if not more than, our physical assets. Additionally, we must also protect the people who are involved in our operations. People are our single most valuable asset, as we cannot generally conduct business without them. We duplicate our physical and logical assets and keep backup copies of them elsewhere against catastrophe occurring, but without the skilled people to operate and maintain our environments, we will swiftly fail.

In our efforts to secure our assets, we must also consider the consequences of the security we choose to implement. There is a well-known quote that says, "The only truly secure system is one that is powered off, cast in a block of concrete and sealed in a lead-lined room with armed guards—and even then I have my doubts" [2]. Although we could certainly say that a system in such a state could be considered reasonably secure, it is surely not usable or productive. As we increase the level of security, we usually decrease the level of productivity. With the system mentioned in our quote, the level of security would be very high, but the level of productivity would be very near zero.

Additionally, when securing an asset, system, or environment, we must also consider how the level of security relates to the value of the item being secured. We can, if we are willing to accommodate the decrease in performance, apply very high levels of security to every asset for which we are responsible. We can build a billion-dollar facility surrounded by razor wire fences and patrolled by armed guards and vicious attack dogs, and carefully place our asset in a hermetically sealed vault inside … so that mom's chocolate chip cookie recipe will never come to harm, but that would not make much sense. In some environments, however, such security measures might not be enough. In any environment where we plan to put heightened levels of security in place, we also need to take into account the cost of replacing our assets if we do happen to lose them, and make sure we establish reasonable levels of protection for their value. The cost of the security we put in place should never outstrip the value of what it is protecting.

When Are We Secure?

Defining the exact point at which we can be considered secure presents a bit of a challenge. Are we secure if our systems are properly patched? Are we secure if we use strong passwords? Are we secure if we are disconnected from the Internet entirely? From a certain point of view, all of these questions can be answered with a "no."

Even if our systems are properly patched, there will always be new attacks to which we are vulnerable. When strong passwords are in use, there will be other avenues that an attacker can exploit. When we are disconnected from the Internet, our systems can be physically accessed or stolen. In short, it is very difficult to define when we are truly secure. We can, however, turn the question around.

Defining when we are insecure is a much easier task, and we can quickly list a number of items that would put us in this state:

- Not patching our systems
- Using weak passwords such as "password" or "1234"
- Downloading programs from the Internet
- Opening e-mail attachments from unknown senders
- Using wireless networks without encryption

We could go on for some time creating such a list. The good thing is that once we are able to point out the areas in an environment that can cause it to be insecure, we can take steps to mitigate these issues. This problem is akin to cutting something in half over and over; there will always be some small portion left to cut again. Although we may never get to a state that we can definitively call "secure," we can take steps in the right direction.

ALERT!

The bodies of law that define standards for security vary quite a bit from one industry to another and wildly from one country to another. Organizations that operate globally are very common at present, and we need to take care that we are not violating any such laws in the course of conducting business. We can see exactly such a case when we look at the differences in data privacy laws between the United States and the European Union. When in doubt, consult legal counsel before acting.

Some bodies of law or regulations do make an attempt to define what secure is, or at least some of the steps we should take to be "secure enough." We have the Payment Card Industry Data Security Standard (PCI DSS) for companies that process credit card payments, the Health Insurance Portability and Accountability Act of 1996 (HIPAA) for organizations that handle health care and patient records, the Federal Information Security Management Act (FISMA) that defines security standards for many federal agencies in the United States, and a host of others. Whether these standards are effective or not is the source of much discussion, but following the security standards defined for the industry in which we are operating is generally considered to be advisable, if not mandated.

MODELS FOR DISCUSSING SECURITY ISSUES

When we discuss security issues, it is often helpful to have a model that we can use as a foundation or a baseline. This gives us a consistent set of terminology and concepts that we, as security professionals, can refer to when security issues arise.

The Confidentiality, Integrity, and Availability Triad

Three of the primary concepts in information security are confidentiality, integrity, and availability, commonly known as the confidentiality, integrity, and availability (CIA) triad, as shown in Figure 1.1. The CIA triad gives us a model by which we can think about and discuss security concepts, and tends to be very focused on security, as it pertains to data.

MORE ADVANCED

The common notation for confidentiality, integrity, and availability is CIA. In certain materials, largely those developed by ISC[2] we may see this rearranged slightly as CAI. No change to the concepts is implied in this rearrangement, but it can be confusing for those who do not know about it in advance. We may also see the CIA concepts expressed in their negative forms: disclosure, alteration, and denial (DAD).

CONFIDENTIALITY

Confidentiality is a concept similar to, but not the same as, privacy. Confidentiality is a necessary component of privacy and refers to our ability to protect our data from those who are not authorized to view it. Confidentiality is a concept that may be implemented at many levels of a process.

As an example, if we consider the case of a person withdrawing money from an ATM, the person in question will likely seek to maintain the confidentiality of the personal identification number (PIN) that allows him, in combination with his ATM card, to draw funds from the ATM. Additionally, the owner of the ATM will hopefully maintain the confidentiality of the account number,

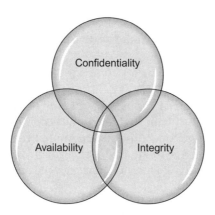

FIGURE 1.1
The CIA Triad

balance, and any other information needed to communicate to the bank from which the funds are being drawn. The bank will maintain the confidentiality of the transaction with the ATM and the balance change in the account after the funds have been withdrawn. If at any point in the transaction confidentiality is compromised, the results could be bad for the individual, the owner of the ATM, and the bank, potentially resulting in what is known in the information security field as a breach.

Confidentiality can be compromised by the loss of a laptop containing data, a person looking over our shoulder while we type a password, an e-mail attachment being sent to the wrong person, an attacker penetrating our systems, or similar issues.

INTEGRITY

Integrity refers to the ability to prevent our data from being changed in an unauthorized or undesirable manner. This could mean the unauthorized change or deletion of our data or portions of our data, or it could mean an authorized, but undesirable, change or deletion of our data. To maintain integrity, we not only need to have the means to prevent unauthorized changes to our data but also need the ability to reverse authorized changes that need to be undone.

We can see a good example of mechanisms that allow us to control integrity in the file systems of many modern operating systems such as Windows and Linux. For purposes of preventing unauthorized changes, such systems often implement permissions that restrict what actions an unauthorized user can perform on a given file. Additionally, some such systems, and many applications, such as databases, can allow us to undo or roll back changes that are undesirable.

Integrity is particularly important when we are discussing the data that provides the foundation for other decisions. If an attacker were to alter the data that contained the results of medical tests, we might see the wrong treatment prescribed, potentially resulting in the death of the patient.

AVAILABILITY

The final leg of the CIA triad is availability. Availability refers to the ability to access our data when we need it. Loss of availability can refer to a wide variety of breaks anywhere in the chain that allows us access to our data. Such issues can result from power loss, operating system or application problems, network attacks, compromise of a system, or other problems. When such issues are caused by an outside party, such as an attacker, they are commonly referred to as a denial of service (DoS) attack.

RELATING THE CIA TRIAD TO SECURITY

Given the elements of the CIA triad, we can begin to discuss security issues in a very specific fashion. As an example, we can look at a shipment of backup tapes on which we have the only existing, but unencrypted, copy of some of our sensitive data stored. If we were to lose the shipment in transit, we will have a security issue. From a confidentiality standpoint, we are likely to have a problem since our files were not encrypted. From an integrity standpoint, presuming that we were able to recover the tapes, we again have an issue due to the lack of encryption used on our files. If we recover the tapes and the unencrypted files were altered, this would not be immediately apparent to us. As for availability, we have an issue unless the tapes are recovered since we do not have a backup copy of the files.

Although we can describe the situation in this example with relative accuracy using the CIA triad, we might find that the model is more restrictive than what we need in order to describe the entire situation. An alternative model does exist that is somewhat more extensive.

The Parkerian Hexad

The Parkerian hexad, named for Donn Parker and introduced in his book *Fighting Computer Crime*, provides us with a somewhat more complex variation of the classic CIA triad. Where the CIA triad consists of confidentiality, integrity, and availability, the Parkerian hexad consists of these three principles, as well as possession or control, authenticity, and utility [3], for a total of six principles, as shown in Figure 1.2.

> **ALERT!**
>
> Although it is considered by some to be a more complete model, the Parkerian hexad is not as widely known as the CIA triad. If we decide to use this model in discussion of a security situation, we should be prepared to explain the difference to the uninitiated.

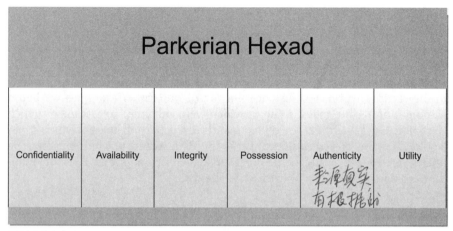

FIGURE 1.2
The Parkerian Hexad

CONFIDENTIALITY, INTEGRITY, AND AVAILABILITY

As we mentioned, the Parkerian hexad encompasses the three principles of the CIA triad with the same definitions we just discussed. There is some variance in how Parker describes integrity, as he does not account for authorized, but incorrect, modification of data, and instead focuses on the state of the data itself in the sense of completeness.

POSSESSION OR CONTROL

Possession or control refers to the physical disposition of the media on which the data is stored. This enables us, without involving other factors such as availability, to discuss our loss of the data in its physical medium. In our lost shipment of backup tapes, let us say that some of them were encrypted and some of them were not. The principle of possession would enable us to more accurately describe the scope of the incident; the encrypted tapes in the lot are a possession problem but not a confidentiality problem, and the unencrypted tapes are a problem on both counts.

AUTHENTICITY

Authenticity allows us to talk about the proper attribution as to the owner or creator of the data in question. For example, if we send an e-mail message that is altered so as to appear to have come from a different e-mail address than the one from which it was actually sent, we would be violating the authenticity of the e-mail. Authenticity can be enforced through the use of digital signatures, which we will discuss further in Chapter 5. A very similar, but reversed, concept to this is nonrepudiation. Nonrepudiation prevents someone from taking an action, such as sending an e-mail, and then later denying that he or she has done so. We will discuss nonrepudiation at greater length in Chapter 5 as well.

UTILITY

Utility refers to how useful the data is to us. Utility is also the only principle of the Parkerian hexad that is not necessarily binary in nature; we can have a variety of degrees of utility, depending on the data and its format. This is a somewhat abstract concept, but it does prove useful in discussing certain situations in the security world. For instance, in one of our earlier examples we had a shipment of backup tapes, some of which were encrypted and some of which were not. For an attacker, or other unauthorized person, the encrypted tapes would likely be of very little utility, as the data would not be readable. The unencrypted tapes would be of much greater utility, as the attacker or unauthorized person would be able to access the data.

ATTACKS

We may face attacks from a wide variety of approaches and angles. When we look at what exactly makes up an attack, we can break it down according to the type of attack that it represents, the risk the attack represents, and the controls we might use to mitigate it.

Types of Attacks

When we look at the types of attacks we might face, we can generally place them into one of four categories: interception, interruption, modification, and fabrication. Each category can affect one or more of the principles of the CIA triad, as shown in Figure 1.3. Additionally, the lines between the categories of attack and the particular effects they can have are somewhat blurry. Depending

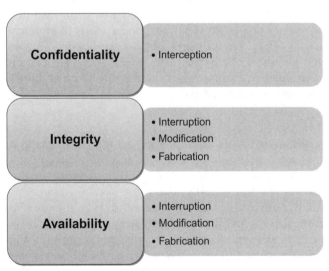

FIGURE 1.3
Categories of Attack

on the attack in question, we might argue for it to be included in more than one category, or have more than one type of effect.

INTERCEPTION

Interception attacks allow unauthorized users to access our data, applications, or environments, and are primarily an attack against confidentiality. Interception might take the form of unauthorized file viewing or copying, eavesdropping on phone conversations, or reading e-mail, and can be conducted against data at rest or in motion. Properly executed, interception attacks can be very difficult to detect.

INTERRUPTION

Interruption attacks cause our assets to become unusable or unavailable for our use, on a temporary or permanent basis. Interruption attacks often affect availability but can be an attack on integrity as well. In the case of a DoS attack on a mail server, we would classify this as an availability attack. In the case of an attacker manipulating the processes on which a database runs in order to prevent access to the data it contains, we might consider this an integrity attack, due to the possible loss or corruption of data, or we might consider it a combination of the two. We might also consider such a database attack to be a modification attack rather than an interruption attack.

DENIAL OF SERVICE

MODIFICATION

Modification attacks involve tampering with our asset. Such attacks might primarily be considered an integrity attack but could also represent an availability attack. If we access a file in an unauthorized manner and alter the data it contains, we have affected the integrity of the data contained in the file. However, if we consider the case where the file in question is a configuration file that manages how a particular service behaves, perhaps one that is acting as a Web server, we might affect the availability of that service by changing the contents of the file. If we continue with this concept and say the configuration we altered in the file for our Web server is one that alters how the server deals with encrypted connections, we could even make this a confidentiality attack.

FABRICATION

Fabrication attacks involve generating data, processes, communications, or other similar activities with a system. Fabrication attacks primarily affect integrity but could be considered an availability attack as well. If we generate spurious information in a database, this would be considered to be a fabrication attack. We could also generate e-mail, which is commonly used as a method for propagating malware, such as we might find being used to spread a worm. In the sense of an availability attack, if we generate enough additional processes, network traffic, e-mail, Web traffic, or nearly anything else that consumes resources, we can potentially render the service that handles such traffic unavailable to legitimate users of the system.

Threats, Vulnerabilities, and Risk

In order to be able to speak more specifically on attacks, we need to introduce a few new items of terminology. When we look at the potential for a particular attack to affect us, we can speak of it in terms of threats, vulnerabilities, and the associated risk that might accompany them.

THREATS

When we spoke of the types of attacks we might encounter, in the "Attacks" section earlier in this chapter, we discussed some of the things that have the potential to cause harm to our assets. Ultimately, this is what a threat is—something that has the potential to cause us harm. Threats tend to be specific to certain environments, particularly in the world of information security. For example, although a virus might be problematic on a Windows operating system, the same virus will be unlikely to have any effect on a Linux operating system.

VULNERABILITIES

Vulnerabilities are weaknesses that can be used to harm us. In essence, they are holes that can be exploited by threats in order to cause us harm. A vulnerability might be a specific operating system or application that we are running, a physical location where we have chosen to place our office building, a data center that is populated over the capacity of its air-conditioning system, a lack of backup generators, or other factors.

RISK

Risk is the likelihood that something bad will happen. In order for us to have a risk in a particular environment, we need to have both a threat and a vulnerability that the specific threat can exploit. For example, if we have a structure that is made from wood and we set it on fire, we have both a threat (the fire) and a vulnerability that matches it (the wood structure). In this case, we most definitely have a risk.

Likewise, if we have the same threat of fire, but our structure is made of concrete, we no longer have a credible risk, because our threat does not have a vulnerability to exploit. We can argue that a sufficiently hot flame could damage the concrete, but this is a much less likely event.

We will often have similar discussions regarding potential risk in computing environments, and potential, but unlikely, attacks that could happen. In such cases, the best strategy is to spend our time mitigating the most likely attacks. If we sink our resources into trying to plan for every possible attack, however unlikely, we will spread ourselves thin and will be lacking in protection where we actually need it the most.

IMPACT

Some organizations, such as the U.S. National Security Agency (NSA), add an additional factor to the threat/vulnerability/risk equation, in the form of impact. If we consider the value of the asset being threatened to be a factor, this may change whether we see a risk as being present or not. If we revisit our example of lost backup tape and stipulate that the unencrypted backup tapes contain only our collection of chocolate chip cookie recipes, we may not actually have a risk. The data being exposed would not cause us a problem, as there was nothing sensitive in it, and we can make additional backups from the source data. In this particular case, we might safely say that we have no risk.

Controls

In order to help us mitigate risk, we can put measures in place to help ensure that a given type of threat is accounted for. These measures are referred to as controls. Controls are divided into three categories: physical, logical, and administrative.

PHYSICAL

Physical controls are those controls that protect the physical environment in which our systems sit, or where our data is stored. Such controls also control access in and out of such environments. Physical controls logically include items such as fences, gates, locks, bollards, guards, and cameras, but also include systems that maintain the physical environment such as heating and air conditioning systems, fire suppression systems, and backup power generators.

Although at first glance, physical controls may not seem like they would be integral to information security, they are actually one of the more critical controls with which we need to be concerned. If we are not able to physically protect our systems and data, any other controls that we can put in place become irrelevant. If an attacker is able to physically access our systems, he can, at the very least, steal or destroy the system, rendering it unavailable for our use in the best case. In the worst case, he will have access directly to our applications and data and will be able to steal our information and resources, or subvert them for his own use.

LOGICAL

Logical controls, sometimes called technical controls, are those that protect the systems, networks, and environments that process, transmit, and store our data. Logical controls can include items such as passwords, encryption, logical access controls, firewalls, and intrusion detection systems.

Logical controls enable us, in a logical sense, to prevent unauthorized activities from taking place. If our logical controls are implemented properly and are successful, an attacker or unauthorized user cannot access our applications and data without subverting the controls that we have in place.

ADMINISTRATIVE

Administrative controls are based on rules, laws, policies, procedures, guidelines, and other items that are "paper" in nature. In essence, administrative controls set out the rules for how we expect the users of our environment to behave. Depending on the environment and control in question, administrative controls can represent differing levels of authority. We may have a simple rule such as "turn the coffee pot off at the end of the day," aimed at ensuring that we do not cause a physical security problem by burning our building down at night. We may also have a more stringent administrative control, such as one that requires us to change our password every 90 days.

One important concept when we discuss administrative controls is the ability to enforce compliance with them. If we do not have the authority or the ability to ensure that our controls are being complied with, they are worse than useless, because they create a false sense of security. For example, if we create a policy that says our business resources cannot, in any fashion, be used for personal use, we need to be able to enforce this. Outside of a highly secure environment, this can be a difficult task. We will need to monitor telephone and mobile phone usage, Web access, e-mail use, instant message conversations, installed software, and other potential areas for abuse. Unless we were willing to devote a great deal of resources for monitoring these and other areas, and dealing with violations of our policy, we would quickly have a policy that we would not be able to enforce. Once it is understood that we do not enforce our policies, we can quickly set ourselves up for a bad situation.

DEFENSE IN DEPTH

Defense in depth is a strategy common to both military maneuvers and information security. In both senses, the basic concept of defense in depth is to formulate a multilayered defense that will allow us to still mount a successful defense should one or more of our defensive measures fail. In Figure 1.4, we can see an example of the layers we might want to put in place to defend our assets from a logical perspective; we would at the very least want defenses at the external network, internal network, host, application, and data levels. Given well-implemented defenses at each layer, we will make it very difficult to successfully penetrate deeply into our network and attack our assets directly.

One important concept to note when planning a defensive strategy using defense in depth is that it is not a magic bullet. No matter how many layers we put in place, or how many defensive measures we place at each layer, we will not be able to keep every attacker out for an indefinite period of time, nor is this the ultimate goal of defense in depth in an information security setting. The goal is to place enough defensive measures between our truly important assets and the attacker so that we will both notice that an attack is in progress and also buy ourselves enough time to take more active measures to prevent the attack from succeeding.

We can see exactly such a strategy in the theater release of the Batman movie, *The Dark Knight*, in 2008. The production company for the movie, Warner Bros., spent six months developing a multilayered defensive strategy to keep the movie from being pirated and placed on file-sharing networks for as long

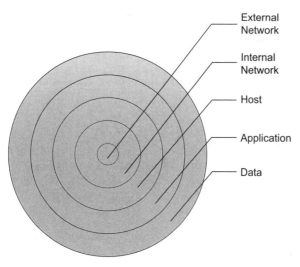

External
Network

Internal
Network

Host

Application

Data

FIGURE 1.4
Defense in Depth

as possible. These measures included a tracking system to monitor who had access to copies of the movie at any given time, shipping the film reels in multiple parts separately to theaters in order to keep the entire movie from being stolen in shipping, monitoring movie theaters with night-vision equipment to watch for those attempting to record the movie in the theater, and other measures. Despite all the time and resources spent to prevent piracy of the movie, it was found on a file-sharing network 38 hours after it was released [4]. For Warner Bros., this was considered a success, as the company was able to prevent the movie from being pirated for a long enough period that opening weekend sales were not significantly impacted.

Layers

When we look at the layers we might place in our defense in depth strategy, we will likely find that they vary given the particular situation and environment we are defending. As we discussed, from a strictly logical information security perspective, we would want to look at the external network, network perimeter, internal network, host, application, and data layers as areas to place our defenses. We could add complexity to our defensive model by including other vital layers such as physical defenses, policies, user awareness and training, and a multitude of others, but we will stay with a simpler example for the time being. As we progress through the book, we will return to the concept of defense in depth as we discuss security for more specific areas.

As we can see in Figure 1.5, some of the defenses we might use for each of the layers we discussed are listed. In some cases, we see a defensive measure listed in multiple layers, as it applies in more than one area. A good example of this is penetration testing. Penetration testing is a method of finding gaps in our

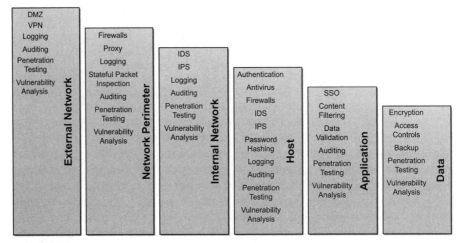

FIGURE 1.5
Defenses in Each Layer

security by using some of the same methods an attacker would use in order to break in (we will discuss this in greater depth in Chapter 6), and is a tactic we might want to use at all layers of our defense. As we move through the book, we will discuss each of these areas in greater detail, and the specific defenses we might want to use for each.

INFORMATION SECURITY IN THE REAL WORLD

The concepts we discussed in this chapter are foundational to information security and are used on a regular basis in the course of normal information security tasks in many organizations. We will often find that security incidents are described in terms of their effects, such as breaches of confidentiality, or the authenticity of a given e-mail message.

Information security is a daily concern for organizations of any size, particularly those that handle any type of personal information, financial data, health-care data, educational data, or other types of data that are regulated by the laws of the country in which they operate. In the case of an organization that does not take the time to properly put itself on a good footing as relates to information security, the repercussions can be severe in the sense of reputational impact, fines, lawsuits, or even the inability to continue conducting business if critical data is irretrievably lost. In short, information security is a key component of the modern business world.

SUMMARY

Information security is a vital component to the era in which data regarding countless individuals and organizations is stored in a variety of computer systems, often not under our direct control. When discussing information security in a general sense, it is important to remember that security and productivity are often diametrically opposing concepts, and that being able to point out exactly when we are secure is a difficult task.

When discussing information security issues or situations, it is helpful to have a model by which to do so. Two potential models are the CIA triad, composed of confidentiality, integrity, and availability, and the Parkerian hexad, composed of confidentiality, integrity, availability, possession or control, authenticity, and utility.

When we look at the threats we might face, it is important to understand the concept of risk. We only face risk from an attack when a threat is present and we have a vulnerability which that particular threat can exploit. In order to mitigate risk, we use three main types of controls: physical, logical, and administrative.

Defense in depth is a particularly important concept in the world of information security. To build defensive measures using this concept, we put in place multiple layers of defense, each giving us an additional layer of protection. The idea behind defense in depth is not to keep an attacker out permanently but to delay him long enough to alert us to the attack and to allow us to mount a more active defense.

EXERCISES

1. Explain the difference between a vulnerability and a threat.
2. List six items that might be considered logical controls.
3. What term might we use to describe the usefulness of data?
4. Which category of attack is an attack against confidentiality?
5. How do we know at what point we can consider our environment to be secure?
6. Using the concept of defense in depth, what layers might we use to secure ourselves against someone removing confidential data from our office on a USB flash drive?
7. Based on the Parkerian hexad, what principles are affected if we lose a shipment of encrypted backup tapes that contain personal and payment information for our customers?
8. If the Web servers in our environment are based on Microsoft's Internet Information Server (IIS) and a new worm is discovered that attacks Apache Web servers, what do we not have?
9. If we develop a new policy for our environment that requires us to use complex and automatically generated passwords that are unique to each system and are a minimum of 30 characters in length, such as *!Hs4(j0qO$ &zn1%2SK38cn^!Ks620!*, what will be adversely impacted?
10. Considering the CIA triad and the Parkerian hexad, what are the advantages and disadvantages of each model?

Bibliography

[1] U.S. Government, Legal Information Institute, Title 44, Chapter 35, Subchapter 111, §3542, Cornell University Law School. <www.law.cornell.edu/uscode/44/3542.html> (accessed: November 22, 2010).

[2] E. Spafford, Quotable spaf, Gene Spafford's personal pages. <http://spaf.cerias.purdue.edu/quotes.html>, 2009 (accessed: November 26, 2010).

[3] D. Parker, Fighting Computer Crime, Wiley, 1998. ISBN: 0471163783.

[4] D. Chmielewski, Secrecy cloaked "Dark Knight," *Los Angeles Times*. <http://articles.latimes.com/2008/jul/28/business/fi-darkknight28>, July 28, 2008 (accessed: November 28, 2010).

CHAPTER 2

Identification and Authentication

Information in This Chapter:
- Identification
- Authentication

INTRODUCTION

When we are developing security measures, whether on the scale of a specific mechanism or an entire infrastructure, identification and authentication are likely to be key concepts. In short, *identification* is the claim of what someone or something is, and *authentication* establishes whether this claim is true. We can see such processes taking place on a daily basis in a wide variety of ways.

One very common example of an identification and authentication transaction can be found in the use of payment cards that require a personal identification number (PIN). When we swipe the magnetic strip on the card, we are asserting that we are the person indicated on the card. At this point, we have given our identification but nothing more. When we are prompted to enter the PIN associated with the card, we are completing the authentication portion of the transaction, hopefully meeting with success.

Some of the identification and authentication methods that we use in daily life are particularly fragile and depend largely on the honesty and diligence of those involved in the transaction. Many such exchanges that involve the showing of identification cards, such as the purchase of items restricted to those above a certain age, are based on the theory that the identification card being displayed is genuine and accurate. We also depend on the person or system performing the authentication being competent and capable of not only performing the act of authentication but also being able to detect false or fraudulent activity.

We can use a number of methods for identification and authentication, from the simple use of usernames and passwords, to purpose-built hardware tokens that serve to establish our identity in multiple ways. We will discuss several of these methods and how they are used throughout the chapter.

IDENTIFICATION

Identification, as we mentioned in the preceding section, is simply an assertion of who we are. This may include who we claim to be as a person, who a system claims to be over the network, who the originating party of an e-mail claims to be, or similar transactions. It is important to note that the process of identification does not extend beyond this claim and does not involve any sort of verification or validation of the identity that we claim. That part of the process is referred to as authentication and is a separate transaction.

Who We Claim to Be

Who we claim to be is a tenuous concept, at best. We can identify ourselves by our full names, shortened versions of our names, nicknames, account numbers, usernames, ID cards, fingerprints, DNA samples, and an enormous variety of other methods. Unfortunately, with a few exceptions, such methods of identification are not unique, and even some of the supposedly unique methods of identification, such as the fingerprint, can be duplicated in many cases.

Who we claim to be can, in many cases, be an item of information that is subject to change. For instance, our names can change, as in the case of women who change their last name upon getting married, people who legally change their name to an entirely different name, or even people who simply elect to use a different name. In addition, we can generally change logical forms of identification very easily, as in the case of account numbers, usernames, and the like. Even physical identifiers, such as height, weight, skin color, and eye color, can be changed. One of the most crucial factors to realize when we are working with identification is that an unsubstantiated claim of identity is not reliable information on its own.

Identity Verification

Identity verification is a step beyond identification, but it is still a step short of authentication, which we will discuss in the next section. When we are asked to show a driver's license, Social Security card, birth certificate, or other similar form of identification, this is generally for the purpose of identity verification, not authentication. This is the rough equivalent of someone claiming the identity "John Smith," us asking if the person is indeed John Smith, and being satisfied with an answer of "Sure I am" from the person (plus a little paperwork). As an identity verification, this is very shaky, at best.

We can take the example a bit further and validate the form of identification—say, a passport—against a database holding an additional copy of the information that it contains, and matching the photograph and physical specifications with the person standing in front of us. This may get us a bit closer, but we are still not at the level of surety we gain from authentication.

Identity verification is used not only in our personal interactions but also in computer systems. In many cases, such as when we send an e-mail, the identity we provide is taken to be true, without any additional steps taken to authenticate us. Such gaps in security contribute to the enormous amount of spam traffic that we see, which is estimated to have accounted for 89.3 percent of all e-mails sent from June to November 2010 [1].

Falsifying Identification

As we have discussed, methods of identification are subject to change. As such, they are also subject to falsification. We have all heard of the commonly used fraudulent driver's license, often used by minors to buy items for which they are too young to purchase, or to get into bars or nightclubs when they are not of age to do so. On a slightly more sinister note, such falsified means of identification are also used by criminals and terrorists for a variety of tasks of a nefarious nature. Certain primary means of identification, such as birth certificates, also provide a way to gain additional forms of identification, such as Social Security cards or driver's licenses, thus strengthening the false identity.

Identity theft, based on falsified information, is a major concern today, costing consumers and businesses an estimated $54 billion in 2009 [2]. This type of attack is unfortunately common and easy to execute. Given a minimal amount of information—usually a name, address, and Social Security number are sufficient—it is possible to impersonate someone to a sufficient degree to be able to act as that person in many cases. Victims of identity theft may find that lines of credit, credit cards, vehicle loans, home mortgages, and other transactions have taken place using their stolen identity.

Such crimes occur due to the lack of authentication requirements for many of the activities in which we engage. In most cases, the only check that takes place is identity verification, as we discussed in the preceding section. This process is a small obstacle, at best, and can easily be circumvented using falsified forms of identification. To rectify this situation, we need to complete the process of identifying and authenticating the people involved in these transactions, in order to at least more conclusively prove that we are actually interacting with the people we believe we are. In the case of individuals, this is not an unsolvable technical problem by any extent, but it is more of a people problem.

When we look at similar issues for computer systems and environments, we can see many of the same difficulties. It is entirely possible to send an e-mail from an address that is different from the actual sending address, and this tactic is used by spammers on a regular basis. We can see the same problems in many other systems and protocols that are in daily use and are part of the functionality of the Internet. We will discuss such issues at greater length in Chapter 8.

AUTHENTICATION

Authentication is, in an information security sense, the set of methods we use to establish a claim of identity as being true. It is important to note that authentication only establishes whether the claim of identity that has been made is correct. Authentication does not infer or imply anything about what the party being authenticated is allowed to do; this is a separate task known as authorization. We will discuss authorization at greater length in Chapter 3, but the important thing to understand for now is that authentication needs to take place first.

Factors

In terms of authentication, there are several methods we can use, with each category referred to as a factor. Within each factor, there are a number of possible methods we can use. When we are attempting to authenticate a claim of identity, the more factors we use, the more positive our results will be. The factors are something you know, something you are, something you have, something you do, and where you are.

Something you know is a very common authentication factor. This can include passwords, PINs, passphrases, or most any item of information that a person can remember. We can see a very common implementation of this in the passwords we use to log in to our accounts on computers. This is somewhat of a weak factor because if the information the factor depends on is exposed, this can nullify the uniqueness of our authentication method.

Something you are is a factor based on the relatively unique physical attributes of an individual, often referred to as biometrics. This factor can be based on simple attributes, such as height, weight, hair color, or eye color, but these do not tend to be unique enough to make very secure identifiers. More commonly used are more complex identifiers such as fingerprints, iris or retina patterns, or facial characteristics. This factor is a bit stronger, as forging or stealing a copy of a physical identifier is a somewhat more difficult, although not impossible, task. There is some question as to whether biometrics truly is an authentication factor, or whether it really only constitutes verification. We will discuss this again later in the chapter when we cover biometrics in greater depth.

Something you have is a factor generally based on the physical possession of an item or a device, although this factor can extend into some logical concepts as well. We can see such factors in general use in the form of ATM cards, state or federally issued identity cards, or software-based security tokens, as shown in Figure 2.1. Some institutions, such as banks, have begun to use access to logical devices such as cell phones or e-mail accounts as methods of authentication as well. This factor can vary in strength depending on the implementation. In the case of a security token, we would actually need to steal a specific device in order to falsify the authentication method. In the case of access to an e-mail address being used as this type of factor, we have a measure of considerably less strength.

FIGURE 2.1
Software Security Token

Something you do, sometimes considered a variation of something you are, is a factor based on the actions or behaviors of an individual. Such factors may include analysis of the individual's gait, measurement of multiple factors in his or her handwriting, the time delay between keystrokes as he or she types a passphrase, or similar factors. These factors present a very strong method of authentication and are very difficult to falsify. They do, however, have the potential to incorrectly reject legitimate users at a higher rate than some of the other factors, resulting in denials for some users that should actually be authenticated.

Where you are is a geographically based authentication factor. This factor operates differently than the other factors, as its method of authentication depends on the person being authenticated as being physically present at a particular location or locations. We can see a somewhat loose implementation of this factor in the act of drawing funds from an ATM. Although this is certainly not a design decision due to security reasons, it is true that this can only be done in particular geographic locations. This factor, although potentially of less utility than some of the other factors, is very difficult to counter without entirely subverting the system performing the authentication.

Multifactor Authentication

Multifactor authentication uses one or more of the factors we discussed in the preceding section. This practice is also referred to, in some cases, as two-factor authentication when we are using only two factors, but multifactor authentication encompasses this term as well.

We can see a common example of multifactor authentication in using an ATM. In this case, we have something we know, our PIN, and something we have, our ATM card. Our ATM card does double duty as both a factor for authentication and a form of identification. We can see a similar example in writing checks that draw on a bank account—in this case, something we have, the checks themselves, and something we do, applying our signature to them. Here, the two factors involved in writing a check are rather weak, so we sometimes see a third factor, a fingerprint, applied to them. We could also argue that the signature and fingerprint are, in this case, not actually authentication, but rather verification, a much less robust process that we discussed when talking about identity earlier in the chapter.

Depending on the particular factors selected, we can assemble stronger or weaker multifactor authentication schemes in a given situation. In some cases, although certain methods may be more difficult to defeat, they are not practical to implement. For example, DNA makes for a very strong method of authentication, but is not practical for regular use. As we discussed in Chapter 1, when discussing security, we need to be careful to build security that is reasonably proportionate to what we are protecting. We could install iris scanners on every credit card terminal instead of having the customer sign his credit card receipt and certainly enhance our security, but this would be expensive and impractical and could upset our customers.

Mutual Authentication

Mutual authentication refers to an authentication mechanism in which both parties authenticate each other. In the standard authentication process, which is one-way authentication only, the client authenticates to the server to prove that it is the party that should be accessing the resources the server provides. In mutual authentication, not only does the client authenticate to the server, but the server authenticates to the client as well. Mutual authentication is often implemented through the use of digital certificates, which we will discuss at greater length in Chapter 5. Briefly, both the client and the server would have a certificate to authenticate the other.

In cases where we do not perform mutual authentication, we leave ourselves open to impersonation attacks, often referred to as man-in-the-middle attacks. In a man-in-the-middle attack, the attacker inserts himself between the client and the server and impersonates the server to the client, and the client to the server, as shown in Figure 2.2. This is done by circumventing the normal pattern of traffic, then intercepting and forwarding the traffic that would normally flow directly between the client and the server. This is typically possible because the attacker only has to subvert or falsify authentication from the client to the server. If we implement mutual authentication, this becomes a considerably more difficult attack to carry out for the attacking party.

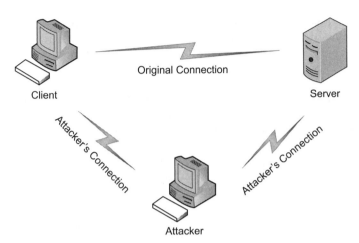

FIGURE 2.2
Man-in-the-Middle Attack

Mutual authentication can also be used in combination with multifactor authentication, with the latter generally taking place on the client side only. Multifactor authentication from the server back to the client would be not only technically challenging but also impractical in most environments. Conceivably, we could implement mutual multifactor authentication in an extremely high security environment, but this would result in a very large loss in productivity.

Passwords

Passwords are familiar to the vast majority of us who use computers regularly. In combination with a username, a password will generally allow us access to a computer system, an application, a phone, or similar devices. Passwords, although only a single factor of authentication, can, when constructed and implemented properly, represent a relatively high level of security.

When we describe a password as being *strong*, we do not provide an immediately accurate image of what we are discussing. A better descriptive term might be *complex* in order to communicate the important concepts inherent to building a password. If we construct a password that is all lowercase letters and is eight characters long, we can use a password-cracking utility, which we will discuss further in Chapter 10, to crack the password in a minute or two, given a reasonably strong computer on which to run the cracking tool. If we use the same eight-character password but use both upper- and lowercase letters, it will take the password cracker around six days to break the password. If we add numbers into the mix, it will take a little more than 25 days to break our password. If we use the recommended password construction method for creating strong passwords, we would create a password that was constructed of uppercase letters, lowercase letters, numbers, and symbols, such as punctuation marks. So, although we would end up with a password that is potentially more difficult to remember, such as *$sU&qw!3*, we would have a password that would take more than two years to crack with an average workstation [3].

MORE ADVANCED

The type of password cracking we are discussing here is called brute force cracking. This involves trying every possible combination of characters that the password could be composed of, in sequence, until we try them all. Given a powerful system on which to run the cracker and a poorly constructed password, this can be a very effective means of recovering passwords. We will discuss this at greater length in Chapter 10.

In addition to constructing strong passwords, we also need to be careful to practice good password hygiene. One problem with strong passwords is that they can be difficult to remember. This might encourage us to take steps to remember our passwords, such as writing them down and posting them in a handy place, perhaps under our keyboard or on our monitor. This, of course, completely defeats the purpose of having a password if someone comes snooping around our desk.

MORE ADVANCED

A number of applications exist, generally under the label of "password managers," that will help us manage all the logins and passwords we have for different accounts, some as locally installed software and some as Web or mobile device applications. There are a number of arguments for and against such tools, but when they are used carefully, they can be of assistance in maintaining good password hygiene.

Another password problem is manual synchronization of passwords—in short, using the same password everywhere. If we use the same password for our e-mail, for our log-in at work, for our online knitting discussion forum, and everywhere else, we are placing the security of all our accounts with each system owner where we use the same password. If any one of them is compromised and its password exposed, we have a serious problem. All an attacker needs to do is look up our account name, *luv2knit*, on the Internet to find some of the places where the same name is used, and start trying our default password. By the time the attacker gets into our e-mail account, the game is over.

Biometrics

When we look at biometrics, we should consider what exactly it is when we use it as an authentication factor. As we discussed in the "Identification" section at the beginning of the chapter, there is a difference between authentication and verification. When we complete an authentication transaction with a biometric identifier, we are essentially asking the user to provide evidence that he or she is who he or she claims to be; this is, by definition, verification, and not authentication. Although some biometric identifiers may be more difficult to falsify than others, this is only due to limitations in today's technology. At some point in the future, we will need to develop more robust biometric characteristics to measure, or stop using biometrics as an authentication mechanism.

ADDITIONAL RESOURCES

Biometrics-equipped devices and readers are becoming common enough that we have begun to see very inexpensive (less than $20) versions of them on the market. It pays to research such devices carefully before we depend on them for security, as some of the cheaper versions are very easily bypassed.

This being said, we can use biometric systems in two different manners. We can use them to verify the claim of identity that someone has put forth, as we discussed earlier, or we can reverse the process and use biometrics as a method of identification. This process is commonly used by law enforcement agencies to identify the owner of fingerprints that have been left on various objects, and can be a very time-consuming effort, considering the sheer size of the fingerprint libraries held by such organizations. We also see similar use in the comparison of DNA samples taken from suspects in crimes compared to physical evidence recovered from the crime scene.

To use a biometric system in either manner, we need to put the user through the enrollment process. Enrollment involves recording the chosen biometric characteristic from the user—for instance, making a copy of a fingerprint—and recording the characteristic in the system. Processing of the characteristic may also include noting certain parts of the image, depending on the characteristic in question, to use for later matching in the system.

CHARACTERISTICS

Biometric factors are defined by seven characteristics: universality, uniqueness, permanence, collectability, performance, acceptability, and circumvention [4].

Universality stipulates that we should be able to find our chosen biometric characteristic in the majority of people we expect to enroll in the system. For instance, although we might be able to use a scar as an identifier, we cannot guarantee that everyone will have a scar. Even if we choose a very common characteristic, such as a fingerprint, we should take into account that some people may not have an index finger on their right hand and be prepared to compensate for this.

Uniqueness is a measure of how unique a particular characteristic is among individuals. For example, if we choose to use height or weight as a biometric identifier, we would stand a very good chance of finding several people in any given group who are of the same height or weight. We can select characteristics with a higher degree of uniqueness, such as DNA, or iris patterns, but there is always a possibility of duplication, whether intentional or otherwise.

Permanence tests show how well a particular characteristic resists change over time and with advancing age. If we choose a factor that can easily vary, such as height, weight, or hand geometry, we will eventually find ourselves in the position of not being able to authenticate a legitimate user. We can instead use factors such as fingerprints that, although they can be altered, are unlikely to be altered without deliberate action.

Collectability measures how easy it is to acquire a characteristic with which we can later authenticate a user. Most commonly used biometrics, such as fingerprints, are relatively easy to acquire, and this is one reason they are in common use. If we choose a characteristic that is more difficult to acquire, such as a footprint, the user will need to remove his shoe and sock in order to enroll (and to authenticate again later), which is considerably more troublesome than taking a fingerprint.

Performance is a set of metrics that judge how well a given system functions. Such factors include speed, accuracy, and error rate. We will discuss the performance of biometric systems at greater length later in this section.

Acceptability is a measure of how acceptable the particular characteristic is to the users of the system. In general, systems that are slow, difficult to use, or awkward to use are less likely to be acceptable to the user [5]. Systems that require users to remove their clothes, touch devices that have been repeatedly used by others, or provide tissue or bodily fluids will likely not enjoy a high degree of acceptability.

Circumvention describes the ease with which a system can be tricked by a falsified biometric identifier. The classic example of a circumvention attack against the fingerprint as a biometric identifier is found in the "gummy finger." In this type of attack, a fingerprint is lifted from a surface, potentially in a covert fashion, and is used to create a mold with which the attacker can cast a positive image of the fingerprint in gelatin. Some biometric systems have features specifically designed to defeat such attacks by measuring skin temperature, pulse, pupillary response, and a number of other items.

MEASURING PERFORMANCE

We can look at many factors when measuring the performance of a biometric system, but a few primary metrics stand out as being particularly important for gauging how well the system is working. False acceptance rate (FAR) and false rejection rate (FRR) are two of these [6]. FAR occurs when we accept a user whom we should actually have rejected. This type of issue is also referred to as a false positive. FRR is the problem of rejecting a legitimate user when we should have accepted him. This type of issue is commonly known outside the world of biometrics as a false negative.

Either of these situations is undesirable in excess. What we try to achieve with such systems is a balance between the two error types, referred to as an equal error rate (EER) [6]. If we plot out both the FAR and FRR on a graph, as we have done in Figure 2.3, the EER is the point where the two lines intersect. EER is sometimes used as a measure of the accuracy of biometric systems.

ISSUES

There are several issues common to biometric systems. As we mentioned when discussing circumvention, some biometric identifiers can be easily forged. Given a falsified identifier, we face a problem; we cannot revoke such a characteristic.

Although we can remove the particular identifier from the system and no longer allow it to be used to authenticate a user, in some cases this is not practical. If we look at fingerprints as an example, we find such a commonly used identifier that someone falsely using our fingerprints could cause us great problems. Although we may currently be able to move to stronger biometrics that, at present, are not easily copied, such as an iris pattern, such efforts will not remain beyond the grasp of attackers forever.

We also face possible issues of privacy in the use of biometrics, both as owners of such systems and as users of them. When we are enrolled in a biometric system, we are essentially giving away a copy of whatever identifier is chosen, whether it is a fingerprint, iris pattern, DNA sample, or otherwise. Once such an item has been entered into a computer system, we have little, if any, control over what is done with the material. We can hope that once we are no longer associated with the institution in question, such materials would be destroyed, but we really have no way of guaranteeing this has actually taken place. Particularly in the case of DNA sampling, the repercussions of surrendering genetic material could be an issue hanging over our heads for the rest of our lives.

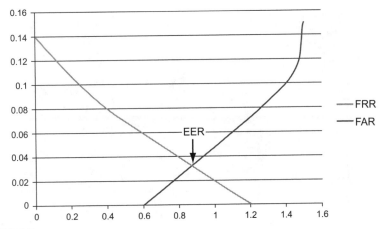

FIGURE 2.3
Equal Error Rate

Hardware Tokens

A standard hardware token is a small device, typically in the general form factor of a credit card or keychain fob. The simplest hardware tokens look identical to a USB flash drive and contain a small amount of storage holding a certificate or unique identifier, and are often called dongles. More complex hardware tokens incorporate LCD displays, as shown in Figure 2.4, keypads for entering passwords, biometric readers, wireless devices, and additional features to enhance security.

Many hardware tokens contain an internal clock that, in combination with the device's unique identifier, an input PIN or password, and potentially other factors, is used to generate a code, usually output to a display on the token. This code changes on a regular basis, often every 30 seconds. The infrastructure used to keep track of such tokens can predict, for a given device, what the proper output will be at any given time, and can use this to authenticate the user.

> **ALERT!**
>
> The simplest variety of hardware tokens represents only the something you have factor and is thus susceptible to theft and potential use by a knowledgeable criminal. Although these devices do represent an increased level of security for the user's accounts, and are generally not useful without the account credentials with which they are associated, we do need to remember to safeguard them.

Hardware tokens represent the something you have authentication factor, sometimes implementing something you know or something you are as well. In the case of simple hardware tokens that only provide the something you have factor, the security provided by the device is only as strong as our ability to prevent it from being stolen, as it could easily be used by an attacker. In the

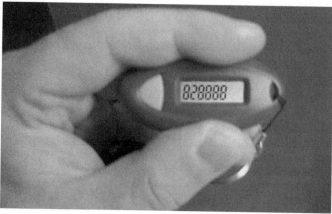

FIGURE 2.4
Hardware Token

case of more complex tokens that include the capability to enter a PIN or read a fingerprint, the security of the device is enhanced considerably. In order for an attacker to utilize a stolen multifactor device, the attacker not only would need the hardware token itself, but also would need to either subvert the infrastructure that was synchronized with the information output from the device, or extract the something you know and/or something you are factor(s) from the legitimate owner of the device.

IDENTIFICATION AND AUTHENTICATION IN THE REAL WORLD

Identification and authentication can be seen at work all over the world on a daily basis. One of the most common examples that we can point out is identity cards, commonly a driver's license in the United States. Such cards are routinely used to prove our identity when making purchases, dealing with government officials and offices, registering for school, and performing a variety of other tasks. In many cases, identification cards are used as a method of verifying our identity while doing these things. Although this is a weak method of verification, it is a commonly used one.

We can see authentication at work when we are carrying out a variety of activities as well. When we use a username and password to log on to a computer at work, or a Web site, we are using the something you know factor. When we enter a PIN and withdraw money from an ATM, we are using the something you know and something you have factors, and we are using multifactor authentication. Many people will not get beyond the use of these two factors in their daily lives.

For those of us who have access to more secure facilities, such as data centers, financial institutions, or military installations, we may see more involved methods of authentication. In some such environments, we will see the use of biometrics, the something you are factor. Many such facilities have moved to the use of iris scanners, now an unobtrusive piece of equipment hanging on the wall near the area to be accessed and only requiring a glance at the lens of the device to proceed. This type of device not only is easy to use but also tends to be more acceptable to users, as we do not need to actually touch it in order for it to work.

We can also see the use of hardware tokens increasing, even for the general public. We can now buy an inexpensive token from VeriSign[A] that will provide an extra layer when we log in to Web sites run by companies such as eBay, PayPal, GEICO, T-Mobile, RadioShack, and hundreds of others. Owing to the large amount of online fraud and identity theft that we see now, any measures that we can use on both personal and organizational levels, such as good password hygiene, strong passwords, and the use of hardware tokens, will help to put us on a stronger security footing all the way around.

[A]https://idprotect.verisign.com/learnmoretoken.v.

SUMMARY

Identification is an assertion of the identity of a particular party. This can be a person, process, system, or other entity. Identification is only a claim of identity and does not imply that this claim is correct, or any privileges that might be associated with the identity, if it is proven true.

Authentication is the process we use to validate whether the claim of identity is correct. It is important to note that authentication and verification are not the same things and that verification is a much weaker test from a security perspective.

When we perform authentication, we can use a number of factors. The main factors are something you know, something you are, something you have, something you do, and where you are. When we use an authentication mechanism that includes more than one factor, this is known as multifactor authentication. Using multiple factors gives us a much stronger authentication mechanism than we might otherwise have.

EXERCISES

1. What is the difference between verification and authentication of an identity?
2. How do we measure the rate at which we fail to authenticate legitimate users in a biometric system?
3. What do we call the process in which the client authenticates to the server and the server authenticates to the client?
4. A key would be described as which type of authentication factor?
5. What biometric factor describes how well a characteristic resists change over time?
6. If we are using an identity card as the basis for our authentication scheme, what steps might we add to the process in order to allow us to move to multifactor authentication?
7. If we are using an 8-character password that contains only lowercase characters, would increasing the length to 10 characters represent any significant increase in strength?
8. Name three reasons why an identity card alone might not make an ideal method of authentication.
9. What factors might we use when implementing a multifactor authentication scheme for users who are logging on to workstations that are in a secure environment and are used by more than one person?
10. If we are developing a multifactor authentication system for an environment where we might find larger-than-average numbers of disabled or injured users, such as a hospital, which authentication factors might we want to use or avoid? Why?

Bibliography

[1] MessageLabs. MessageLabs intelligence: November 2010, <http://www.messagelabs.com/mlireport/MLI_2010_11_November_FINAL.pdf>, 2010.

[2] Javelin Strategy, 2010 Identity fraud survey report, <http://www.javelinstrategy.com/research/brochures/Brochure-170>, 2010.

[3] I. Lucas, Password recovery speeds, Lockdown.co.uk. <http://www.lockdown.co.uk/?pg=combi>, July 10, 2009 (accessed: December 1, 2010).

[4] A.K. Jain, A. Ross, S. Prabhakar, An introduction to biometric recognition, IEEE Trans. Circuits Syst. Video Technol. 14 (1) (2004).

[5] A. Patrick, Usability and acceptability of biometric security systems, Lect. Notes Comput. Sci. 3110 (105) (2004), doi: 10.1007/978-3-540-27809-2_11.

[6] V. Matyás Jr., Z. Riha, Toward reliable user authentication through biometrics, IEEE Secur. Privacy 1 (3) (2003). ISSN: 1540-7993.

CHAPTER 3

Authorization and Access Control

Information in This Chapter:

- Authorization
- Access Control
- Access Control Methodologies

INTRODUCTION

Once we have received a claim of identity and established whether that claim is valid, as we discussed in Chapter 2, we move on to what the party is allowed to do and whether we will allow or deny them access to our resources. We can achieve this with two main concepts: authorization and access control. Authorization allows us to specify where the party should be allowed or denied access, and access control enables us to manage this access at a very granular level.

Access controls can be constructed in a variety of manners. We can base access controls on physical attributes, sets of rules, lists of individuals or systems, or more complex factors. The particular type of access control often depends on the environment in which it is to be used. We can find simpler access controls implemented in many applications and operating systems, while more complex multilevel configurations might be implemented in military or government environments. In such cases, the importance of what we are controlling access to may dictate that we track what our users have access to across a number of levels of sensitivity.

When we discuss access control concepts, we may be referring to them in a purely logical or physical sense or, more commonly, as a combination of the two. In terms of access control systems, it is important to understand that, when dealing with computing environments, the logical and physical are often closely entangled. Logical access control systems, even those that do not have an immediately obvious physical component, are still dependent on physical hardware, networks, and utilities to carry out their tasks. Likewise, many, but not all, physical access controls (sometimes referred to as guards, gates, and guns) have some sort of logical component. Often the systems that control our access to and within facilities depend equally on networks, computer systems, and other similar components. In many ways, information security and physical security are closely linked to each other.

AUTHORIZATION

Authorization is the next step taken after we have completed identification and authentication, as shown in Figure 3.1. Authorization enables us to determine, once we have authenticated the party in question, exactly what they are allowed to do. We typically implement authorization through the use of access controls, which we will discuss later in this chapter.

Principle of Least Privilege

When we are determining what access we will provide to the parties to whom we have provided authorized access, there is an important concept we should keep in mind, called the principle of least privilege. The principle of least privilege dictates that we should only allow the bare minimum of access to a party—this might be a person, user account, or process—to allow it to perform the functionality needed of it. For example, someone working in a sales department should not need access to data in our internal human resources system in order to do their job. Violation of the principle of least privilege is the heart of many of the security problems we face today.

One of the more common ways in which we find the principle of least privilege improperly implemented is in the permissions we give operating system (OS) user accounts, most commonly violated by users and administrators of Microsoft operating systems. In Microsoft operating systems, we will often find that casual users of the OS, who are performing tasks such as creating documents in word processors and exchanging e-mail, are configured with administrative access, thus allowing them to carry out any task that the OS allows. As a consequence of this, whenever the overprivileged user opens an e-mail attachment containing malware, or encounters a Web site that pushes attack code to the client computer, these attacks have free reign on the system because they are acting as the user, who is, in turn, endowed with administrative capabilities. Because of this, the attacker's job is much easier, as they can simply turn

FIGURE 3.1
Identification, Authentication, and Authorization

off anti-malware tools, install any additional attack tools they care to, and proceed with completely compromising the system.

We can see the same issue in services or processes that are running at a more privileged level than they need to in order to carry out their functions. If we have a service running a Web server, for instance, this service only needs sufficient permission to access the files and scripts that directly pertain to the Web content it is serving, and nothing more. If we allow the Web service to access additional files in the file system, an attacker could potentially read or alter these files to gain unauthorized access to more sensitive information than we would normally make public, thus giving the attacker an inroad to attack deeper into the system.

By carefully following the principle of least privilege when configuring systems, allocating permissions for accounts, and planning out our security, we can take away some of the more easily accessed tools that attackers can use against us. This is a very simple security measure that we can put in place, and it is very effective.

ACCESS CONTROL

When we look at access controls we have four basics tasks we might want to carry out: allowing access, denying access, limiting access, and revoking access. Among these four actions, we can describe most access control issues or situations.

Allowing access lets us give a particular party, or parties, access to a given resource. For example, we might want to give a particular user access to a file, or we may want to give an entire group of people access to all the files in a given directory. We might also be referring to access in a physical sense, by giving our employees access to our facility through the use of a key or badge.

Denying access is the diametric opposite of granting access. When we deny access we are preventing access by a given party to the resource in question. We might be denying access to a particular person attempting to log on to a machine based on the time of day, or we might deny unauthorized individuals from entering the lobby of our building beyond business hours. Many access control systems are set to deny by default, with the authorized users only being permitted access.

Limiting access refers to allowing some access to our resource, but only up to a certain point. This is very important when we are using applications that may be exposed to attack-prone environments, as we see with Web browsers used on the Internet. In such cases, we might see the application being run in a sandbox in order to limit what can be done outside the context of the application. In a physical sense, we can see the concept of access control limitations in the different levels of keying that we might see in the locks in a building. We may have a master key that can open any door in the building, an intermediate key that can open only a few doors, and a low-level key that can open only one door.

> **MORE ADVANCED**
>
> When we look at limiting the access for software, we will often see the term *sandbox* used to describe the limitations that are put in place. A sandbox is simply a set of resources devoted to a program, process, or similar entity, outside of which the entity cannot operate. We use sandboxes to prevent their contents from accessing files, memory, and other system resources with which they should not be interacting. Sandboxes can be very useful for containing things that we cannot trust, such as code from public Web sites. We can see an example of a sandbox in use in the Java Virtual Machine (JVM) under which programs written in the Java programming language run. The JVM is specifically constructed to protect users against potentially malicious software that they might download.

Revocation of access is a very important idea in access control. It is vital that once we have given a party access to a resource, we be able to take that access away again. If we were, for instance, to fire an employee, we would want to revoke any accesses that they might have. We would want to remove access to their e-mail account, disallow them from connecting to our virtual private network (VPN), deactivate their badge so that they can no longer enter the facility, and revoke other accesses that they might have. Particularly when we are working with computer-oriented resources in some fashion, it may be vital to be able to revoke access to a given resource very quickly.

When we look to implement access controls, there are two main methods that we might use: access control lists and capabilities. Each of these has positives and negatives, and the ways we can carry out the four basic tasks we covered earlier will differ depending on the method we choose for our access control implementation.

Access Control Lists

Access control lists (ACLs), often referred to as "ackles," are a very common choice of access control implementation. ACLs are usually used to control access in the file systems on which our operating systems run and to control the flow of traffic in the networks to which our systems are attached.

When ACLs are constructed, they are typically built specifically to a certain resource, and they contain the identifiers of the party allowed to access the resource in question and what the party is allowed to do in relation to the resource. As we see in Figure 3.2, Alice is allowed access to the resource, while Bob is specifically denied access. This may seem like a very simplistic concept, but in the context of larger ACL implementations, such as those used in file systems, ACLs can become quite complex.

FILE SYSTEM ACLs

When we look at the ACLs in most file systems, we commonly see three permissions in use: read, write, and execute, respectively allowing us to access the

Alice	Allow
Bob	Deny

FIGURE 3.2
A Simple ACL

contents of a file or directory, write to a file or directory, and, presuming that a file contains either a program or a script capable of running on the system in question, execute the contents of the file.

In the case of file systems, a file or directory may also have multiple ACLs attached to it. In UNIX-like operating systems, for instance, we can see separate access lists for a given file, in the form of *user*, *group*, and *other* ACLs. We can give an individual user read, write, and execute permissions, a group of users different read, write, and execute permissions, and a different set of read, write, and execute permissions to anyone that is not an individual or group that we have already covered. These three sets of permissions will display as *rwxrwxrwx*, with the first *rwx* set representing the *user*, the second the *group*, and the third *other*, as shown in Figure 3.3.

MORE ADVANCED

To further explore the idea, we can look at the specific example of one of the files shown in Figure 3.3. If we look at the first file, .nano_history, we can see that the permissions are displayed as - *r w* - - - - - - -. This may seem a bit cryptic, but we can help this somewhat by segmenting this into the relevant sections. If we divide it as - | *r w* - | - - - | - - -, we can see where the different sections lie. The first - is generally used to represent the file type. In the case of our example, - represents a regular file, and *d* represents a directory. The second segment, the user permissions, is set to *r w* -, meaning that the user that owns the file can read it and write it, but not execute it. The third segment, the group permissions, is set to - - -, meaning that the members of the group that owns the file cannot read it, write it, or execute it. The last segment is also set to - - -, meaning that anyone that is not the user that owns the file or in the group that owns the file can also not read, write, or execute it.

By using such sets of file permissions, we can, in a simple fashion, control access to the operating systems and applications that utilize our file system. Although we only looked at file system permissions like these as they pertain to file systems used in Microsoft and UNIX-like operating systems, most file systems use a very similar, if not identical, set of permissions.

```
root@bt: ~ - Shell - Konsole
Session  Edit  View  Bookmarks  Settings  Help
-rw-------  1 root root          1 Aug   4 23:23 .nano_history
drwxr-xr-x  2 root root       4096 Oct   1 19:13 .netbeans
drwx------  2 root root       4096 Oct   4 19:30 .openvas
-rw-------  1 root root        709 Oct   4 19:30 .openvasrc
-rw-r--r--  1 root root        282 Aug   4 17:43 .profile
drwxr-xr-x  2 root root       4096 May 10  2009 .qt
-rw-------  1 root root       1024 Oct   4 12:46 .rnd
drwxr-xr-x  3 root root       4096 May  9  2010 .subversion
drwxr-xr-x  3 root root       4096 May 28  2009 .wine
-rw-------  1 root root        192 May 10  2009 .xcompmgrrc
-rw-------  1 root root      77473 Dec 12 11:39 .xsession-errors
-rw-r--r--  1 root root          0 Nov 10 17:52 00
-rw-r--r--  1 root root       2200 Oct   1 19:22 0d32d0e.jpg
-rw-r--r--  1 root root          0 Nov 10 17:52 10
-rw-r--r--  1 root root          0 Nov 10 17:52 11
-rw-r--r--  1 root root          0 Nov 10 17:52 17
-rw-r--r--  1 root root          0 Nov 10 17:52 2010
-rw-r--r--  1 root root       7158 Oct   1 19:28 35858185
-rw-r--r--  1 root root          0 Nov 10 17:52 45
-rwxr-xr-x  1 root root         41 Jun 16  2009 install.sh
-rwxr-xr-x  1 root root  156620358 Oct   4 12:38 metasploit-3.5.0-beta-linux-insta
ller.bin
-rw-r--r--  1 root root          0 Nov 10 17:52 test
root@bt:~#
  Shell
```

FIGURE 3.3
File Permissions on a Linux Operating System

NETWORK ACLs

When we look at the variety of activities that take place on networks, both private and public, we can again see ACLs regulating such activity. In the case of network ACLs, we typically see access controlled by the identifiers we use for network transactions, such as Internet Protocol (IP) addresses, Media Access Control (MAC) addresses, and ports. We can see such ACLs at work in network infrastructure such as routers, switches, and firewall devices, as well as in software firewalls, Facebook, Google, e-mail, or other forms of software.

Permissions in network ACLs tend to be binary in nature, generally consisting of allow and deny. When we set up the ACL, we use our chosen identifier or identifiers to dictate which traffic we are referring to and simply state whether the traffic is to be allowed or not.

One of the simplest forms of network-oriented ACLs that we might see in place is MAC address filtering. MAC addresses are, in theory, unique identifiers attached to each network interface in a given system. Each network interface has a hardcoded MAC address issued when it is created.

ALERT!

Unfortunately for those of us depending on MAC addresses as a basis for our ACLs, the MAC address used by a network interface can be overridden by software settings in most operating systems. Such changes are very trivial to put in place, and the MAC address is not a good choice for a unique identifier of a particular device on the network.

We can also choose to use IP addresses as the basis for filtering in our ACL. We can implement such filtering based on individual addresses, or on an entire range of IP addresses. Unfortunately, similar to the issue with using MAC addresses for ACLs, IP addresses can be falsified and are not unique to a particular network interface. Additionally, IP addresses issued by Internet service providers (ISPs) are subject to frequent change, making IP addresses as the sole basis for filtering a shaky prospect, at best.

MORE ADVANCED

Some organizations, such as those that operate Web servers, mail servers, and other services that are exposed to the Internet, apply large-scale filtering in order to block out known attacks, spammers, and other undesirable traffic. Such filtering can take the form of dropping traffic from individual IP addresses, to ranges, to the entire IP space of large organizations, ISPs, or even entire countries. This practice is commonly referred to as blackholing, because any traffic to such filtered destinations is simply dropped and appears to have vanished into a black hole from the perspective of the sender.

We can also filter by the port being used to communicate over the network. Many common services and applications use specific ports to communicate over networks. For instance, FTP uses ports 20 and 21 to transfer files, Internet Message Access Protocol (IMAP) uses port 143 for managing e-mail, Secure Shell (SSH) uses port 22 to manage remote connections to systems, and many more—65,535 ports in all. We can control the use of many applications over the network by allowing or denying traffic originating from or sent to any ports that we care to manage. Like MAC and IP addresses, the specific ports that are used for applications are a convention, not an absolute rule. We can, with relative ease, change the ports that applications use to different ports entirely.

Using single attributes to construct ACLs is likely to present a variety of issues, including our attribute not being guaranteed to be unique, such as an IP address, or being easy to alter, such as a MAC address. When we use several attributes in combination we begin to arrive at a more secure technique. A very commonly used combination is that of IP address and port, typically referred to as a socket. In this way, we can allow or deny network traffic from one or more IP addresses using one or more applications on our network in a workable fashion.

We can also construct ACLs to filter on a wide variety of other things. In some cases, we might want to monitor the traffic going over our network in order to allow or deny traffic based on more specific criteria, such as the content of an individual packet or a related series of packets. Using such techniques, we can filter out traffic related to attacks, or traffic that is simply undesirable to us, such as that related to the peer-to-peer file-sharing networks commonly used to illegally share copyrighted songs, videos, and software.

Capabilities

Capability-based security can provide us with an alternate solution to access control that uses a different structure than what we see in ACLs. Where ACLs define the permissions based on a given resource, an identity, and a set of permissions, all generally held in a file of some sort, capabilities are oriented around the use of a token that controls our access. We can think of a token in a capability as being analogous to the badge we might use to open the door in a building. We have one door, and many people have a token that will open it, but we can have differing levels of access. Where one person might be able to access the building only during business hours on weekdays, another person may have permission to enter the building at any time of day on any day of the week.

Interestingly, in capability-based systems, the right to access a resource is based entirely on possession of the token, and not who possesses it. As with our badge example, if we were to give our badge to someone else, he would be able to use it to access the building with whatever set of permissions we have. In a capability-based system, applications can share with other applications the token that defines their level of access. In noncapability-based systems, which use ACLs to manage permissions, we may experience the confused deputy problem, due to the way that access control is implemented.

CONFUSED DEPUTY PROBLEM

The confused deputy problem is a type of attack that is common in systems that use ACLs rather than capabilities. The crux of the confused deputy problem is seen when the software with access to a resource has a greater level of permission to access the resource than the user who is controlling the software. If we, as the user, can trick the software into misusing its greater level of authority, we can potentially carry out an attack [1]. We will discuss a few practical examples of attacks that exploit the confused deputy problem later in this section.

Several specific attacks, many of them client side in nature, can take practical advantage of the confused deputy problem. These often involve tricking the user into taking some action when they really think they are doing something else entirely. Two of the more common uses of such an attack are client-side attacks such as cross-site request forgery (CSRF) and clickjacking.

Client-side attacks are attacks that take advantage of weaknesses in applications that are running on the computer being operated directly by the user, often referred to as the client. These attacks can take the form of code sent through the Web browser, which is then executed on the local machine, malformed PDF files, images or videos with attack code embedded, or other forms. In the past several years, software vendors have become more aware of such attacks as an issue and have begun building defensive measures into their software, but new attacks appear on a regular basis.

CSRF is an attack that misuses the authority of the browser on the user's computer. If the attacker knows of, or can guess, a Web site to which the user might already be authenticated, perhaps a very common site such as Amazon.com, he can attempt to carry out a CSRF attack [2]. He can do this by embedding a link in a Web page or HTML-based e-mail, generally a link to an image from the site to which he wishes to direct the user without their knowledge. When the application attempts to retrieve the image in the link, it also executes the additional commands the attacker has embedded in it. In our example, when the user's browser loads the image from Amazon.com, as long as the authentication cookie for Amazon has not expired, the attacker might cause the user to make a purchase without their knowledge, thus allowing the attacker to sell more copies of a book.

Clickjacking, also known as user interface redressing, is a particularly sneaky and effective client-side attack that takes advantage of some of the page rendering features that are available in newer Web browsers. In order to carry out a clickjacking attack, the attacker must legitimately control or have taken control of some portion of the Web site that is to be used as the attack vehicle. The attacker constructs or modifies the site in order to place an invisible layer over something the client would normally click on, in order to cause the client to execute a command differing from what they actually think they are performing [3]. Clickjacking can be used to trick the client into making purchases, changing permissions in their applications or operating systems, or performing other nefarious activities.

If we were to use capabilities instead of ACLs to manage permissions, these attacks would not be possible. In the case of each of these attacks, the misuse of permissions would not be possible, because the attacker would not be able to misuse the authority of the user without actually having access to the token that would allow him permission to do so.

ALERT!

Browser attacks are very common and are likely to succeed against systems that have not been hardened against them specifically. Some of the more commonly used browsers, such as Microsoft's Internet Explorer and Mozilla Firefox, now include at least a rudimentary form of protection against such attacks. Browser security plug-ins, such as NoScript[A] for Firefox and GuardedID[B] for Internet Explorer, can also help to foil such attacks.

[A]http://noscript.net/
[B]www.guardedid.com/default.aspx

Unfortunately, the most commonly used operating systems have only a very minimal implementation of capability-based security, and this does not often extend to the sharing of permissions between applications. In most cases, in order to mitigate the attacks that we discussed, additional layers of security, in the form of applications or plug-ins, are needed.

ACCESS CONTROL METHODOLOGIES

Access controls are the means by which we implement authorization and deny or allow access to parties, based on what resources we have determined they should be allowed access to. Although the term may sound very technical and oriented in the direction of high-security computing facilities, access controls are something we deal with on a daily basis.

When we lock or unlock the doors on our house, we are using a form of physical access control, based on the keys (something you have) that we use.

When we start our car, we are also likely to use a key. For some newer cars, our key may even include an extra layer of security by adding Radio Frequency Identification (RFID) tags, certificate-like identifiers stored on the key itself, and other security technologies.

Upon reaching our place of employment, we might use a badge (something you have) to enter the building, once again, a physical access control.

When we sit down in front of our computer at work and type in our password (something you know), we are authenticating and using a logical access control system in order to access the resources to which we have been given permission. Depending on the environments we pass through in the course of working, going to school, and performing the other activities that make up our day, we may have more or less exposure to access controls, but most of us see multiple implementations like these on a regular basis.

Access Control Models

There are quite a few different access control models we might run across, and we will cover the most common models here. The most likely set we will encounter in the security world includes discretionary access control, mandatory access control, rule-based access control, role-based access control, and attribute-based access control.

DISCRETIONARY ACCESS CONTROL

Discretionary access control (DAC) is a model of access control based on access being determined by the owner of the resource in question. The owner of the resource can decide who does and does not have access, and exactly what access they are allowed to have. In Microsoft operating systems, we can see DAC implemented. If we decide to create a network share, for instance, we get to decide who we want to allow access.

MANDATORY ACCESS CONTROL

Mandatory access control (MAC) is a model of access control in which the owner of the resource does not get to decide who gets to access it, but instead access is decided by a group or individual who has the authority to set access on resources. We can often find MAC implemented in government organizations, where access to a given resource is largely dictated by the sensitivity label applied to it (secret, top secret, etc.), by the level of sensitive information the individual is allowed to access (perhaps only secret), and by whether the individual actually has a need to access the resource, as we discussed when we talked about the principle of least privilege earlier in this chapter.

> **MORE ADVANCED**
>
> It is worthwhile to note that MAC is an overloaded acronym, in that it can have more than one meaning. In this case, two of the more common meanings are Media Access Control (MAC), as in the unique identifier for a network interface, and mandatory access control (MAC), in the sense of a type of access control.

ROLE-BASED ACCESS CONTROL

Role-based access control (RBAC) is a model of access control that, similar to MAC, functions on access controls set by an authority responsible for doing so, rather than by the owner of the resource. The difference between RBAC and MAC is that access control in RBAC is based on the role the individual being granted access is performing. For example, if we have an employee whose only role is to enter data into a particular application, through RBAC we would only allow the employee access to that application, regardless of the sensitivity or lack of sensitivity of any other resource he might potentially access. If we have an employee with a more complex role—customer service for an online retail application, perhaps—the employee's role might require him to have access to information about customers' payment status and information, shipping status, previous orders, and returns, in order to be able to assist said customers. In this case, RBAC would grant him considerably more access. We can see RBAC implemented in many large-scale applications that are oriented around sales or customer service.

ATTRIBUTE-BASED ACCESS CONTROL

Attribute-based access control (ABAC) is, logically, based on attributes. These can be the attributes of a particular person, of a resource, or of an environment.

Subject attributes are those of a particular individual. We could choose any number of attributes, such as the classic "you must be this tall to ride" access control, which exists to prevent the altitudinally challenged from riding on amusement park rides that might be harmful to them. Another very common example can be seen in the use of a Captcha, as shown in Figure 3.4. Captchas are used to control access, based on whether the party on the other end can pass a test that is, in theory, too difficult for a machine to complete, thus proving the party to be human. Captcha or, more properly, CAPTCHA, stands for Completely Automated Public Turing Test to Tell Humans and Computers Apart [4].

condition welorta

FIGURE 3.4
A Captcha

Resource attributes are those that relate to a particular resource, such as an operating system or application. We often see this occur, although usually for technical reasons rather than security reasons, when we encounter software that only runs on a particular operating system, or Web sites that only work with certain browsers. We might apply this type of access control as a security measure by requiring specific software to be used or particular protocols for communication.

Environmental attributes can be used to enable access controls that operate based on environmental conditions. We commonly use the time attribute to control access, in both a physical and a logical sense, based on length of time passed, or time of day. Access controls on buildings are often configured to only allow access during certain hours of the day, such as during business hours. We also see time limits set on VPN connections, forcing the user to reconnect every 24 hours. This is often done to prevent users from keeping such a connection running after their authorization for using it has been removed. We can often find ABAC implemented on infrastructure systems such as those in network or telecommunications environments.

MULTILEVEL ACCESS CONTROL

Multilevel access control models are used where the simpler access control models that we just discussed are considered to not be robust enough to protect the information to which we are controlling access. Such access controls are used extensively by military and government organizations, or those that often handle data of a very sensitive nature. We might see multilevel security models used to protect a variety of data, from nuclear secrets to protected health information (PHI).

The Bell-LaPadula model implements a combination of DAC and MAC access controls, and is primarily concerned with the confidentiality of the resource in question. Generally, in cases where we see DAC and MAC implemented together, MAC takes precedence over DAC, and DAC works within the accesses allowed by the MAC permissions. For example, we might have a resource that is classified as secret and a user that has a secret level of clearance, normally allowing them to access the resource under the accesses allowed by MAC. However, we might also have an additional layer of DAC under the MAC access, and if the resource owner has not given the user access, they would not be able to access it, despite the MAC permissions. In Bell-LaPadula, we have two security properties that define how information can flow to and from the resource [5]:

- *The Simple Security Property*: The level of access granted to an individual must be at least as high as the classification of the resource in order for the individual to be able to access it.

- *The *Property*: Anyone accessing a resource can only write its contents to one classified at the same level or higher.

These properties are generally summarized as "no read up" and "no write down," respectively. In short, this means that when we are handling classified information, we cannot read any higher than our clearance level, and we cannot write classified data down to any lower level.

The Biba model of access control is primarily concerned with protecting the integrity of data, even at the expense of confidentiality. Biba has two security rules that are the exact reverse of those we discussed in the Bell-LaPadula model [6]:

- *The Simple Integrity Axiom:* The level of access granted to an individual must be no lower than the classification of the resource.
- *The *Integrity Axiom:* Anyone accessing a resource can only write its contents to one classified at the same level or lower.

We can summarize these rules as "no read down" and "no write up," respectively. This may seem completely counterintuitive when we consider protecting information, but remember that we have changed the focus from confidentiality to integrity. In this case, we are protecting integrity by ensuring that our resource can only be written to by those with a high level of access and that those with a high level of access do not access a resource with a lower classification.

The Brewer and Nash model, also known as the Chinese Wall model, is an access control model designed to prevent conflicts of interest. Brewer and Nash is commonly used in industries that handle sensitive data, such as that found in the financial, medical, or legal industry. Three main resource classes are considered in this model [7]:

- *Objects*: Resources such as files or information, pertaining to a single organization.
- *Company groups*: All objects pertaining to a particular organization.
- *Conflict classes*: All groups of objects that concern competing parties.

If we look at the example of a commercial law firm working for companies in a certain industry, we might have files that pertain to various individuals and companies working in that industry. As an individual lawyer at the firm accesses data and works for different clients, he could potentially access confidential data that would generate a conflict of interest in him while working on a new case. In the Brewer and Nash model, the resources and case materials that the lawyer was allowed access to would dynamically change based on the materials he had previously accessed.

Physical Access Controls

Many of the access control methods we have discussed throughout the chapter can be applied to physical security as well as logical security. When concerned with physical access controls, we are often largely concerned with controlling the access of individuals and vehicles.

Access control for individuals often revolves around controlling movement into and out of buildings or facilities. We can see simple examples of such controls on the buildings of many organizations in the form of badges that moderate opening doors into or within the facility (something you have, from Chapter 2). Such badges are typically configured on an ACL that permits or denies their use for certain doors and regulates the time of day that they can be used.

One of the more common issues with physical access controls is that of tailgating. Tailgating occurs when we authenticate to the physical access control measure, such as using a badge, and then another person follows directly behind us without authenticating themselves. Tailgating can cause a variety of issues, including allowing unauthorized individuals into the building and creating an inaccurate representation of who is actually in the building in case there is an emergency.

We can attempt to solve tailgating in a variety of ways, from implementing policy that forbids doing so, to posting a guard in the area, to simply (but expensively) installing a physical access control solution that only allows one person to pass through at a time, such as a turnstile. All of these are reasonable solutions, but, depending on the environment in question, may or may not be effective. We will often find that a combination of several solutions is needed to develop a thorough and complete solution.

A much more complex example of this type of access control that many people are familiar with is the security system in use at many airports. Particularly after the terrorist attacks of 9/11 in the United States, we have seen the level of security at airports increase, much of it oriented in the direction of access controls. Once we have entered the airport security system, we are required to present a boarding pass and identification (something you have, times two). We are then typically passed through a number of steps to ensure that we do not carry any dangerous devices, a form of attribute-based access control. We then proceed to our gate and, once again, present our boarding pass to step onto the airplane. Such processes may differ slightly depending on the country in which we travel, but they are generally the same from an access control perspective.

Physical access control for vehicles often revolves around keeping said vehicles from moving into or through areas in which we do not desire them to be. This is often done through the use of various simple barriers, including Jersey barriers such as those shown in Figure 3.5, bollards, one-way spike strips, fences, and similar tools. We may also see more complex installations that include manned or unmanned rising barriers, automated gates or doors, and other similar items.

There are, of course, a huge number of other physical access controls and methods that we have not discussed here. Additionally, when we refer to physical access control devices, or access controls in general, the line between what is an authentication device and an access control device often becomes rather blurry.

FIGURE 3.5
A Jersey Barrier [8]

AUTHORIZATION AND ACCESS CONTROL IN THE REAL WORLD

We can see authorization and access control used in our personal and business lives on an almost constant basis, although the portions of these that are immediately visible to us are the access controls. Looking specifically at logical access controls, we can see them used when we log in to computers or applications, when we send traffic over the Internet, when we watch cable or satellite television, when we make a call on our mobile phones, and in thousands of other places. In some cases, such measures are visible to us and require us to enter a password or a PIN, but a large portion of them happen in the background, completely invisible to the tasks we are carrying out and taken care of by the technologies that facilitate our tasks.

In the sense of physical access controls, we see these rather frequently as well, although it may not register to us that we are seeing them. Most of us carry around a set of keys that allow us access to our homes, cars, and other devices, and these are the credentials for access to them. Many of us also carry proximity badges that allow us access to our places of employment, schools, and other areas. We can also see the access controls that manage the movement of vehicles in everyday use in vehicle-oriented areas such as parking garages and parking areas at airports, and in the vicinity of high-security areas such as the White House in the United States.

SUMMARY

Authorization is a key step in the process that we work through in order to allow entities access to resources, namely, identification, authentication, and authorization, in that order. We implement authorization through the use of access controls, more specifically through the use of access control lists and capabilities, although the latter are often not completely implemented in most of the common operating systems in use today.

The specifics of access control are defined through the various models we use when putting together such systems. We often see the use of the simpler access control models such as discretionary access control, mandatory access control, role-based access control, and attribute-based access control in our daily lives. In environments that handle more sensitive data, such as those involved in the government, military, medical, or legal industry, we may see the use of multi-level access control models, including Bell LaPadula, Biba, Clark-Wilson, and Brewer and Nash.

Access control concepts in general largely apply to both logical and physical areas, but we do see some specialized applications when looking specifically at physical access control. Here we have several sets of access controls that apply to ensuring that people and vehicles are restricted from exiting or entering areas where they are not authorized to be. We can see examples of such controls in our daily lives at office buildings, parking areas, and high-security facilities in general.

EXERCISES

1. Discuss the difference between authorization and access control.
2. What does the Clark-Wilson model protect against?
3. Why does access control based on the MAC address of the systems on our network not represent strong security?
4. Which should take place first, authorization or authentication?
5. What are the differences between MAC and DAC in terms of access control?
6. The Bell-LaPadula and Biba multilevel access control models each have a primary security focus. Can these two models be used in conjunction?
7. Given a file containing sensitive data and residing in a Linux operating system, would setting the permissions to *rw-rw-rw-* cause a potential security issue? If so, which portions of the CIA triad might be affected?
8. Which type of access control would be used in the case where we wish to prevent users from logging in to their accounts after business hours?
9. Explain how the confused deputy problem can allow privilege escalation to take place.
10. What are some of the differences between access control lists and capabilities?

Bibliography

[1] N. Hardy, The confused deputy: (or why capabilities might have been invented), ACM SIGOPS Oper. Syst. Rev. 22 (4) (1988). ISSN: 0163-5980.

[2] K.J. Higgins, CSRF vulnerability: a 'sleeping giant.' Dark Reading. <www.darkreading.com/security/application-security/208804131/index.html>, October 17, 2006 (accessed: December 12, 2010).

[3] F. Callegati, M. Ramilli, Frightened by links, IEEE Secur. Privacy 7 (6) (2009). ISSN: 1540-7993.

[4] L. von Ahn, M. Blum, J. Langford, Telling humans and computers apart automatically, Commun. ACM 47 (2) (2004).

[5] L.J. LaPadula, D.E. Bell, Secure Computer Systems: Mathematical Foundations, vol. l, Mitre Corporation, 1973.

[6] K.J. Biba, Integrity Considerations for Secure Computer Systems, Mitre Corporation, 1975.

[7] T.Y. Lin, Chinese wall security policy—an aggressive model, Fifth Annual Computer Security Applications Conference, 1989.

[8] Maryland Department of Transportation State Highway Administration, Jersey barrier in place on southbound I-95/I-495. Maryland Department of Transportation State Highway Administration, <http://apps.roads.maryland.gov/WebProjectLifeCycle/ProjectPhotos.asp?projectno=PG5725116#>, 2010.

CHAPTER 4

Auditing and Accountability

Information in This Chapter:

- Accountability
- Auditing

INTRODUCTION

When we have successfully gone through the process of identification, authentication, and authorization, or even while we are still going through the process, we need to keep track of the activities that have taken place, as shown in Figure 4.1. Even though we might have allowed the party access to our resources, we still need to ensure that they behave in accordance with the rules as they relate to security, business conduct, ethics, sexual harassment, and so on.

In recent years, being able to ensure that we, and those that use our environments, are abiding by the rules set forth for use has become a vital task. We now house a great deal of information in digital form, including medical data, financial information, legal proceedings, trade secrets, and a variety of other items. If we do not set, and follow, stringent rules for access to sensitive data stored in this fashion, we can suffer business losses, intellectual property theft, identity theft, fraud, and numerous other crimes. Some types of data—medical and financial, for example—often enjoy protection by law in a number of countries. In the United States, two such well-known bodies of law are found in the Health Information Portability and Accountability Act of 1996 (HIPAA) and the Sarbanes–Oxley Act of 2002 (SOX), protecting medical and financial data, respectively.

Many of the measures we put in place to ensure accountability fall under the general heading of auditing. We perform audits to ensure that compliance with applicable laws, policies, and other bodies of administrative control is being accomplished. We may audit a variety of activities, including compliance with policy, proper security architecture, application settings, personal behavior, or other activities or configurations.

FIGURE 4.1
Accountability

ACCOUNTABILITY

Accountability provides us with the means to trace activities in our environment back to their source. In addition, it provides us with a number of capabilities, when properly implemented, which can be of great use in conducting the daily business of security and information technology in our organizations. In particular, organizations need to carefully maintain accountability in order to ensure that they are in compliance with any laws or regulations associated with the types of data they handle, or the industry in which they operate.

To ensure that we have accountability, we need certain other tools to be in place and working properly. Accountability depends on identification, authentication, and access control being present so that we can know who a given transaction is associated with, and what permissions were used to allow them to carry it out. Given proper monitoring and logging, we can often do exactly this and determine, in very short order, the details of the situation in question.

It is very easy to look at accountability and the associated auditing tools that are commonly attached to it and dismiss them as being bad because they are akin to Big Brother watching over our shoulder. In some senses, this is true, and excessive monitoring of people, places, and things can indicate an unhealthy environment. We can also go too far in the other direction. If we do not have sufficient controls in place to deter or prevent those that would break the rules and abuse the resources they have access to, we can end up in a bad place as well.

If we consider the example of the Enron scandal in 2001, we can see a case where, due to lack of accountability to its shareholders, board of directors, auditors, and the U.S. government, Enron was able to defraud its investors out of billions of dollars. This was one of the events that prompted the enactment of SOX, directed specifically at halting such practices. In some cases, such as these, accountability equates to a certain extent to transparency. In some situations, our activities must be transparent to certain parties, such as shareholders, in order to hold us accountable for our actions. Such transparency is dictated by law in companies that are publicly traded.

We may also see cases where accountability is prompted by outside agencies, but the impetus to comply with these requirements must come from within our organizations. We can see an example of this in the requirements for notifying those that have had personal or financial information exposed in an unauthorized manner in a security breach. Such breaches seem to happen with disturbing regularity, and we can generally find a current example of one through a brief search of the news media. When a company experiences a breach in the United States, it will often be required, by law, to notify those whose information has been exposed. In many cases, however, the breaches are not known of outside the company by more than a very few people, until they are actually announced to those that are directly involved. We can certainly see where such an organization might be tempted, in such a case, to not say anything about the incident.

> ### MORE ADVANCED
> In the United States, 46 states, the District of Columbia, Puerto Rico, and the U.S. Virgin Islands have, at the time of this writing, laws in place that dictate notification to those whose personally identifiable information (PII) has been involved in a breach. Presently, the only states that do not are Alabama, Kentucky, New Mexico, and South Dakota [1].

Although the breach may not be immediately visible to those outside the organization, or ever visible, for that matter, we are still accountable to be compliant with the laws that govern breaches in our location and with any laws that govern the handling of the data with which we conduct business. In the case where we do not conduct ourselves properly as relates to these laws, we may be able to continue with business as usual for a period of time, but we will eventually be discovered and the repercussions in the personal, business, and legal senses will be much greater for not having handled the situation properly in the first place.

Security Benefits of Accountability

Implementing accountability often brings with it a number of useful features from a security perspective. When we implement monitoring and logging on our systems and networks, we can use this information to maintain a higher security posture than we would be able to otherwise. Specifically, the tools that allow us accountability also enable nonrepudiation, deter those that would misuse our resources, help us in detecting and preventing intrusions, and assist us in preparing materials for legal proceedings.

NONREPUDIATION

Nonrepudiation refers to a situation in which sufficient evidence exists as to prevent an individual from successfully denying that he or she has made a statement, or taken an action. In information security settings, this can be accomplished in a variety of ways. We may be able to produce proof of the activity directly from system or network logs, or recover such proof through the use of digital forensic examination of the system or devices involved. We may also be able to establish nonrepudiation through the use of encryption technologies, more specifically through the use of hash functions that can be used to digitally sign a communication or a file. We will discuss such methods at considerably greater length in Chapter 5 when we go over encryption. An example of this might be a system that digitally signs every e-mail that is sent from it, thus rendering useless any denial that might take place regarding the sending of the message in question.

DETERRENCE

Accountability can also prove to be a great deterrent against misbehavior in our environments. If those we monitor are aware of this fact, and it has been communicated to them that there will be penalties for acting against the rules, these individuals may think twice before straying outside the lines.

MORE ADVANCED

The key to deterrence lies in letting those we want to deter know they will be held accountable for their actions. This is typically carried out through the vehicle of auditing and monitoring, both of which we will discuss in the "Auditing" section of this chapter. If we do not make this clear, our deterrent will lose most of its strength.

For example, if, as part of our monitoring activities, we keep track of the badge access times for when our employees pass in and out of our facility, we can validate this activity against the times they have submitted on their time card for each week, in order to prevent our employees from falsifying their time card and defrauding the company for additional and undeserved pay. While this might seem to smack of Big Brother to some (as, perhaps, it should), such methods are often used in areas with large numbers of employees working specific shifts, such as those that run technical support help desks.

INTRUSION DETECTION AND PREVENTION

One of the motivations behind logging and monitoring in our environments is to detect and prevent intrusions in both the logical and physical sense. If we implement alerts based on unusual activities in our environments and check the information we have logged on a regular basis, we stand a much better chance of detecting attacks that are in progress and preventing those for which we can see the precursors.

Particularly in the logical realm where attacks can take place in fractions of a second, we would also be wise to implement automated tools to carry out such tasks. We can divide such systems into two major categories: intrusion detection systems (IDSes) and intrusion prevention systems (IPSes). An IDS performs strictly as a monitoring and alert tool, only notifying us that an attack or undesirable activity is taking place. An IPS, often working from information sent by the IDS, can actually take action based on what is happening in the environment. In response to an attack over the network, an IPS might refuse traffic from the source of the attack. We will discuss IDSes and IPSes at greater length in Chapters 7, 8, and 10.

ADMISSIBILITY OF RECORDS

When we seek to introduce records in legal settings, it is often much easier to do so and have them accepted when they are produced from a regulated and consistent tracking system. For instance, if we seek to submit digital forensic evidence that we have gathered for use in a court case, the evidence will likely not be admissible to the court unless we can provide a solid and documented chain of custody for said evidence. We need to be able to show where the evidence was at all times, how exactly it passed from one person to another, how it was protected while it was stored, and so forth.

Our accountability methods for evidence collection, if properly followed, will hopefully let us display this unbroken chain of custody. If we cannot demonstrate this, our evidence will likely only be taken as hearsay, at best, considerably weakening our case, and perhaps placing us on the losing side in court.

How We Accomplish Accountability

As we have discussed, we can attempt to ensure accountability by laying out the rules and ensuring that they are being followed. While it is all well and good to give someone a rule and ask him or her to follow it, we will often need to take further steps to ensure that this is actually taking place. We can see exactly such a mechanism at work in the law enforcement world. The geographical area in which we live has laid out certain laws for its populace to follow. Often, we can find laws governing theft, harm to others, safe operation of vehicles, and many more. We then have police that ensure compliance with these laws, in both a reactive and a proactive way. In the world of information security, we often use the tools of technology to carry out similar tasks.

AUDITING

One of the primary ways we can ensure accountability through technical means is by ensuring that we have accurate records of who did what and when they did it. In nearly any environment, from the lowest level of technology to the highest, accountability is largely accomplished through the use of auditing of some variety. *Merriam-Webster's Dictionary of Law* defines an audit as "a methodical examination and review" [2].

We audit for one of several reasons. Auditing provides us with the data with which we can implement accountability. If we do not have the ability to assess our activities over a period of time, we do not have the ability to facilitate accountability on a large scale. Particularly in larger organizations, our capacity to audit directly equates to our ability to hold anyone accountable for anything.

We may also be bound by contractual or regulatory requirements that compel us to be subject to audit on some sort of reoccurring basis. In many cases, such audits are carried out by unrelated and independent third parties certified and authorized to perform such a task. Good examples of such audits are those mandated by SOX, which exist in order to ensure that companies are honestly reporting their financial results.

What Do We Audit?

When we perform an audit there are a number of items we can examine, primarily focused on compliance with relevant laws and policies. In the information security world, we tend to look at access to or from systems as a primary focus, but often extend this into other fields as well, such as physical security.

Passwords are a commonly audited item, as we should be setting out policy to dictate how they are constructed and used. As we discussed in "Authentication" section in Chapter 2, if we do not take care to construct passwords in a secure manner, they can be easily cracked by an attacker. We should also be concerned with the frequency at which passwords are changed. If we do happen to have a password fall into the hands of someone who should not have it, we want to change the password at a relatively frequent interval in order to ensure that this person does not have permanent access. In many cases, checking password strength and managing password changes are accomplished in an automated fashion by functions within an operating system or by utilities designed to do so, and these need to be audited as well to ensure that they are in place and configured properly.

Software licensing is another common audit topic. Particularly on systems owned by the organization for which we work, ensuring that all of our software is appropriately licensed is an important task. If we were to be audited by an outside agency—the Business Software Alliance (BSA), for instance—and we were found to be running large quantities of unlicensed software, the financial penalties could be severe indeed. It is often best if we can find and correct such matters ourselves before receiving a notification from an external company such as the BSA.

> **ALERT!**
>
> The BSA is a company that, on behalf of software companies (Adobe or Microsoft, for instance), regularly audits other companies to ensure their compliance with software licensing. Fines from the BSA can reach $250,000 *per occurrence* of unlicensed software, and the BSA sweetens the pot for whistle-blowers by offering rewards of up to $1 million for reporting violations [3].

Internet usage is a very commonly audited item in organizations, often largely focused on our activities on the Web, although it may include instant messaging, e-mail, file transfers, or other transactions. In many cases, organizations have configured proxy servers so that all such traffic is funneled through just a few gateways in order to enable logging, scanning, and potentially filtering such traffic. Such tools can give us the ability to examine how exactly such resources are being utilized and to take action if they are being misused.

Many organizations, as we have mentioned throughout this chapter, handle data of a sensitive nature. Particularly in the case of data that is required by law to be protected, medical data being a good example, we must take steps to ensure that we are complying with any security measures we are required to have in place. In particular, we are often bound to ensure that accesses to such data are carried out in an authorized fashion, that any requirements for data retention over a period of time are met, and that the data is safely destroyed when it is no longer needed. Such data is often housed in some variety of database, most of which have built-in facilities for controlling and monitoring access on a very granular level.

Logging

Logging gives us a history of the activities that have taken place in the environment being logged. We typically generate logs in an automated fashion in operating systems, and keep track of the activities that take place on most computing, networking, and telecommunications equipment, as well as most any device that can be remotely considered to incorporate or be connected to a computer. Logging is a reactive tool, in that it allows us to view the record of what happened after it has taken place. In order to immediately react to something taking place, we would need to use a tool more along the lines of an IDS/IPS.

Logging mechanisms are often configurable and can be set up to log anything from solely critical events, which is typical, to every action carried out by the system or software, which is typically only done for troubleshooting purposes when we see a problem. We will often find events such as software errors, hardware failures, users logging in or out, resource access, and tasks requiring increased privileges in most logs, depending on the logging settings and the system in question.

Logs are generally only available to the administrators of the system for review and are usually not modifiable by the users of the system, perhaps with the exception of writing to them. It is very important to note that collecting logs without reviewing them is a fairly futile task. If we never review the content of the logs, we might as well have not collected them in the first place. It is important that we schedule a regular review of our logs in order to catch anything unusual in their contents.

We may also be asked to analyze the contents of logs in relation to a particular incident or situation. These types of activities often fall to security personnel in the case of investigations, incidents, and compliance checks. In these cases, this can be a difficult task if the period of time in question is greater than a few days. Even searching the contents of a relatively simple log, such as that generated by a Web proxy server, can mean sifting through enormous amounts of data from one or more servers. In such cases, custom scripts or even a tool such as grep can be invaluable to accomplish such tasks in a reasonable amount of time.

Monitoring

Monitoring is a subset of auditing and tends to focus on observing information about the environment being monitored in order to discover undesirable conditions such as failures, resource shortages, security issues, and trends that might signal the arrival of such conditions. Monitoring is largely a reactive activity, with actions taken based on gathered data, typically from logs generated by various devices. Although we might consider the trend analysis portion of logging to be a proactive activity, we are still reacting to the present circumstances in order to forestall worse conditions than those we see at present.

When conducting monitoring we are typically watching specific items of data we have collected, such as resource usage on computers, network latency, particular types of attacks occurring repeatedly against servers with network interfaces that are exposed to the Internet, traffic passing through our physical access controls at unusual times of day, and so forth. In reaction to such activity occurring at levels above what we normally expect, called the clipping level, our monitoring system might be configured to send an alert to a system administrator or physical security personnel, or it might trigger more direct action to mitigate the issue such as dropping traffic from a particular IP address, switching to a backup system for a critical server, summoning law enforcement officials, or other similar tasks.

Assessments

In some cases, our audits may take a more active route toward determining whether everything is as it should be and compliant with the relevant laws, regulations, or policies. In such cases, we may find it useful to carefully examine our environments for vulnerabilities. We can take two main approaches to such activities: vulnerability assessments and penetration testing. While these terms are often used interchangeably, they are actually two distinct sets of activities.

Vulnerability assessments generally involve using vulnerability scanning tools, such as Nessus,[A] as shown in Figure 4.2, in order to locate such vulnerabilities. Such tools generally work by scanning the target systems to discover which ports are open on them, and then interrogating each open port to find out exactly which service is listening on the port in question. Given this information, the vulnerability assessment tool can then consult its database of vulnerability information to determine whether any vulnerabilities may be present. Although the databases of such tools do tend to be rather thorough, newer attacks or those that are used very sparingly by attackers will often escape their notice.

[A] http://www.nessus.org/

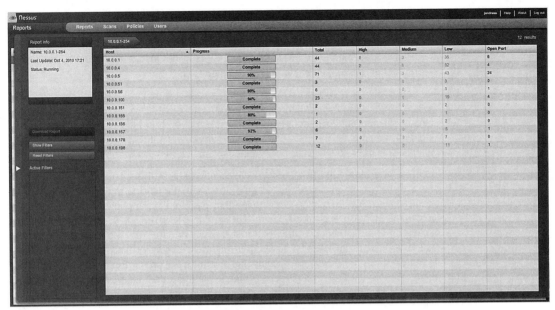

FIGURE 4.2
Nessus

As a more active method of finding security holes, we may also wish to conduct penetration testing. Penetration testing, although it may use vulnerability assessment as a starting place, takes the process several steps further. When we conduct a penetration test, we mimic, as closely as possible, the techniques an actual attacker would use. We may attempt to gather additional information on the target environment from users or other systems in the vicinity, exploit security flaws in Web-based applications or Web-connected databases, conduct attacks through unpatched vulnerabilities in applications or operating systems, or similar methods. We will discuss penetration testing at greater length in Chapters 8, 9, and 10.

The ultimate goal in performing assessments of either type is to find and fix vulnerabilities before any attackers do. If we can do so successfully and on a reoccurring basis, we will considerably increase our security posture and stand a much better chance of resisting attacks. As with any security measure that we can put in place, security assessments are only a single component in our overall defensive strategy.

ACCOUNTABILITY AND AUDITING IN THE REAL WORLD

Accountability and auditing are commonly seen to some extent in the regular activities most of us carry out. When we examine our encounters with accountability, we can see that they take place with great regularity. We are held accountable for our compliance with local and national laws for the geographic areas in which we are located;

likewise, for the policies and regulations laid out by our employers, schools, banks, and any of hundreds of other entities with which we do business of some variety. We also hold others accountable for their actions on the other side of the transaction. We want those that handle our information to protect it, our leadership to be honest and live up to their stated goals and policies, and so forth.

For nearly any action we might care to take, an associated audit record is created or updated in a computer system somewhere. Our medical histories, grades in school, purchases, credit history, and an enormous number of other factors are regularly queried and updated by the individuals and organizations with which we have contact. Such data is used to make decisions that can impact our lives for better or worse.

Audit data is also used, whether it focuses on our activities as an individual or on the activities of organizations, to mitigate attacks that might be taking place. We can see an example of this in the monitoring that credit card companies conduct on the purchases made through our account. For instance, if we decide to buy half a dozen laptops in one day, chances are good that this will deviate from the normal purchase habits of most of us. In such cases, this will often trigger an alert in the monitoring systems run by the credit card company, and will temporarily freeze any purchases made with our card. The credit card company will more than likely attempt to contact us to ensure that the transaction is legitimate before allowing it to proceed. Such efforts quietly take place in the background around us all the time.

SUMMARY

When we allow others to access the resources on which our businesses are based, or personal information of a sensitive nature, we need to hold them accountable for what they do with the resources or information. Accountability may be a requirement for organizations, depending on the data they deal with and the industry in which they operate.

Auditing is the process we go through to ensure that our environment is compliant with the laws, regulations, and policies that bind it. Auditing is also the mechanism through which we can implement accountability. We may carry out a variety of tasks in the name of auditing, including logging, monitoring, assessments, and the like.

In order to support auditing, accountability, and monitoring activities, we often conduct logging on many of the devices in our environment. Such logs are often generated by software, computing devices, and other hardware connected to computers. Logs generated by devices can be very general in nature and contain only a limited amount of information, or they can be very specific and contain large amounts of highly detailed information.

Based on the data we collect from systems, we can also conduct monitoring in our environments. Monitoring allows us to take action on activities in the period after they have happened, potentially ranging from identifying trends in the operation of our systems to taking action to block attacks very quickly after they have first been identified.

EXERCISES

1. What is the benefit of logging?
2. Discuss the difference between authentication and accountability.
3. Describe nonrepudiation.
4. Name five items we might want to audit.
5. Why is accountability important when dealing with sensitive data?
6. Why might auditing our installed software be a good idea?
7. When dealing with legal or regulatory issues, why do we need accountability?
8. What is the difference between vulnerability assessment and penetration testing?
9. What impact can accountability have on the admissibility of evidence in court cases?
10. Given an environment containing servers that handle sensitive customer data, some of which are exposed to the Internet, would we want to conduct a vulnerability assessment, a penetration test, or both? Why?

Bibliography

[1] National Conference of State Legislatures, State Security Breach Notification Laws, National Conference of State Legislatures. <http://www.ncsl.org/default.aspx?tabid=13489>, October 12, 2010 (accessed: December 14, 2010).

[2] Merriam-Webster's Dictionary of Law, Audit. Dictionary.com. <http://dictionary.reference.com/browse/audit>, 2011 (accessed: February 21, 2011).

[3] Business Software Alliance, Faces of Internet Piracy. <http://portal.bsa.org/faces/pdf/FOIP-pr.pdf>, 2010 (accessed: December 14, 2010).

CHAPTER 5
Cryptography

Information in This Chapter:

- History
- Modern Cryptographic Tools
- Protecting Data at Rest, in Motion, and in Use

INTRODUCTION

The use of cryptography is an integral part of computing, networking, and the vast set of transactions that take place over such devices on a daily basis. We use cryptography when we have conversations on our cell phones, check out e-mail, buy things from online retailers, file our taxes, and do other activities. The chief security measure that allows us to make use of such technologies is cryptography—in the form of encryption. If we were not able to utilize encryption to protect the information we send over such channels, many of the Internet-based activities we enjoy today would be carried out at a much greater risk than they are carried out presently.

To discuss cryptography properly, it is helpful to first have a good understanding of the terms used to describe encryption, its components, and the people involved in its development and use.

Cryptography, practiced by cryptographers, is the science of keeping information secure (secure, in this case, in the sense of confidentiality and integrity; refer back to our discussion in Chapter 1). Cryptography is also commonly and interchangeably referred to as encryption. Encryption itself is actually a subset of cryptography, referring specifically to the transformation of unencrypted data, called plaintext or cleartext, into its encrypted form, called ciphertext. Decryption is the process of recovering the plaintext message from the ciphertext. The plaintext and ciphertext may also be generically referred to as the message.

The science of breaking through the encryption used to create the ciphertext is referred to as cryptanalysis and is practiced by cryptanalysts. The overarching field of study that covers cryptography and cryptanalysis is referred to as cryptology and is practiced by cryptologists.

The specifics of the process used to encrypt the plaintext or decrypt the ciphertext is referred to as a cryptographic algorithm. Cryptographic algorithms generally use a key, or multiple keys, in order to encrypt or decrypt the message, this being roughly analogous to a password. The range of all possible values for the key is referred to as the keyspace. We may also refer to the cryptosystem, a concept that covers a given algorithm and all possible keys, plaintexts, and ciphertexts.

HISTORY

History is rich with the use of cryptography, with some of the oldest examples being used by the ancient Greeks and Romans. Information was hidden by a wide variety of codes, by tattooing them on the shaved heads of messengers and then allowing the hair to grow, and by a multitude of other methods. Enough historical information exists to fill an entire volume, and indeed many books have been written on the subject, but we will go over just a few quick highlights.

Caesar Cipher

The Caesar cipher is a classic example of ancient cryptography and is said to have been used by Julius Caesar. The Caesar cipher involves shifting each letter of the plaintext message by a certain number of letters, historically three, as shown in Figure 5.1. The ciphertext can be decrypted by applying the same number of shifts in the opposite direction. This type of encryption is known as a substitution cipher, due to the substitution of one letter for another in a consistent fashion.

A more recent variation of the Caesar cipher can be found in the ROT13 cipher. ROT13 uses the same mechanism as the Caesar cipher but moves each letter 13 places forward. The convenience of moving 13 places lies in the fact that applying another round of encryption with ROT13 also functions as decryption, as two rotations will return us to the original starting place in the alphabet. Utilities for performing ROT13 can be found in the basic set of tools that ship with many Linux and UNIX operating systems.

S	E	C	R	E	T	M	E	S	S	A	G	E
V	H	F	U	H	W	P	H	V	V	D	J	H

FIGURE 5.1
Caesar Cipher

Cryptographic Machines

Before the advent of the modern computer, machines existed that simplified the use of encryption and made more complex encryption schemes feasible. Initially, such devices were simple mechanical machines, but as technology progressed, we began to see the inclusion of electronics and considerably more complex systems.

The Jefferson Disk, invented by Thomas Jefferson in 1795, is a purely mechanical cryptographic machine. It is composed of a series of disks, each marked with the letters a to z around its edge, as shown in Figure 5.2.

On each disk, the letters are arranged in a different order; each disk is also marked with a unique designator to facilitate arranging them in a particular order. The device built by Jefferson contained 36 disks, with each disk representing one character in the message. In order to encrypt a message, we would line up the characters in a row across the set of disks to create the message in plaintext, as shown in row A of Figure 5.3, and then choose a different row of characters to use as the ciphertext, as shown in row B.

The key to this form of cipher is in the order of the disks. As long as the encrypting and decrypting devices have disks with the characters in the same order, and the disks themselves are in the same order, all we need to do to decrypt the message is to line up the disks in the same order as the ciphertext, and then look over the rows to find the plaintext message. This is, of course, merely a more complex version of a substitution cipher, made possible through the use of a mechanical aid.

FIGURE 5.2
Jefferson Disk [1]

	A	F	T	K	D	A	R	X	Z	X	Z	X
	B	K	O	E	E	Q	U	T	Y	U	I	A
	P	I	P	Q	U	W	Z	W	V	Y	U	C
	I	L	Y	G	L	B	C	V	D	Z	P	R
	U	Q	G	B	M	K	W	B	T	W	F	U
	L	A	L	D	A	R	N	U	E	P	E	P
	H	V	C	O	Z	P	M	N	W	S	L	Q
A	M	E	E	T	I	N	G	I	S	A	G	O
	X	C	H	W	V	U	O	S	M	O	Y	J
	O	U	Z	N	Y	H	B	E	X	T	D	B
	E	Z	A	P	N	F	Q	M	U	B	A	G
	V	J	U	X	F	J	I	C	P	E	N	F
	Y	G	R	L	Q	E	A	L	L	K	S	W
	C	Y	M	V	P	O	P	G	K	C	O	D
	G	M	K	A	B	G	S	A	I		H	V
	X	W	N	M	W	I	F	D	F	N	R	L
	K	D	F	U	J	D	T	R	B	D	L	M
	F	O	W	H	R	M	J	Q	H	G	X	E
	S	X	N	I	S	T	E	K	O	R	M	Y
	D	B	D	Y	G	V	Y	F	Q	V	T	H
	R	H	Q	Z	K	S	L	J	A	I	J	S
B	T	N	J	R	O	C	H	O	N	L	Q	I
	Q	P	I	F	C	X	K	P	G	F	V	N
	J	R	B	S	X	Z	D	Z	C	M	W	K
	W	S	V	J	H	L	V	H	J	J	B	Z
	N	T	G	C	P	Y	X	Y	R	Q	C	T

FIGURE 5.3
Jefferson Disk Layout

FIGURE 5.4
German Enigma I [2]

A more intricate example of a cryptographic machine can be found in the German-made Enigma machine. The Enigma was created by Arthur Scherbius in 1923 and was used to secure German communications during World War II. In fact, there were several models of Enigma machine, and a variety of accessories and add-ons that could be attached to them. The particular machine in Figure 5.4 is a later model, the Enigma I, which was developed in 1932.

The Enigma was based on a series of wheels, referred to as rotors, each with 26 letters and 26 electrical contacts on them, similar in general concept to the Jefferson Disk. The device also had a keyboard, on which the plaintext message was entered, and a set of 26 characters above the keyboard, each of which could be lit. To add further possible variations, some models also had a patch panel, allowing some or all the letters to be swapped by plugging cables into different positions. On each rotor, the ring containing the letters of the alphabet could also be rotated independently of the electrical contacts, in order to change the relationship between the character selected and the character output.

MORE ADVANCED

For anyone interested in getting hands-on experience with a classic item of cryptographic history that the Enigma represents, there are several modern options. For the DIY inclined, a kit is available that re-creates the functionality of the Enigma using modern electronics components.[A] Additionally, a variety of software-based Enigma simulators exist.[B] Software simulators are particularly instructive in showing a visual representation of the relationships between the rotors and how the path through them changes with each character entered.

[A]www.cryptomuseum.com/kits/enigma/desc.htm
[B]http://enigmaco.de

When a key was pressed on the keyboard, one or more of the rotors would physically rotate, depending on its configuration, thereby changing the orientation of the electrical contacts between the rotors. Current would flow through the entire series of disks, and then back through them again to the original disk. The scrambled equivalent of the letter would light on the series of characters above the keyboard and be recorded.

In order for two Enigma machines to communicate, they needed to be configured identically. The rotors needed to be the same and in the same position, the rings marked with the alphabet on each rotor needed to be in the same position, the rotors needed to be set to the same starting position, and any plugs in the plugboard needed to be configured in the same fashion. Between the inherent strengths of the device and the knowledge of the required configuration needed for decryption, the Enigma posed quite a difficult task for those attempting to break the messages generated by it.

ADDITIONAL RESOURCES

A great many books have been written on this topic, but a particularly good one is *The German Enigma Cipher Machine: Beginnings, Success, and Ultimate Failure* from Artech House (ISBN-13: 9781580539968).

Kerckhoffs' Principle

In 1883, the *Journal des Sciences Militaires* published an article by Auguste Kerckhoffs titled "la cryptographie militaire." In the article, Kerckhoffs outlined six principles around which a cryptographic system should be based [3]:

1. The system must be substantially, if not mathematically, undecipherable.
2. The system must not require secrecy and can be stolen by the enemy without causing trouble.
3. It must be easy to communicate and remember the keys without requiring written notes, and it must be easy to change or modify the keys with different participants.

4. The system ought to be compatible with telegraph communication.

5. The system must be portable, and its use must not require more than one person.

6. Finally, regarding the circumstances in which such system is applied, it must be easy to use and must require neither the stress of mind nor the knowledge of a long series of rules.

Although several of these principles have become outmoded with the advent of computers to aid in cryptography, the second principle has become a tenet of cryptographic algorithms. This idea was later restated by Claude Shannon as "the enemy knows the system" [4]. Both versions of this concept mean that cryptographic algorithms should be robust enough that, even though someone may know every bit of the system with the exception of the key itself, he or she should still not be able to break the encryption. This idea represents the opposite approach to "security through obscurity" and is one of the underlying principles for many modern cryptographic systems.

MODERN CRYPTOGRAPHIC TOOLS

Although very efficient electromechanical cryptographic systems existed, such as the Enigma that enables a highly secure means of communication for a period of time, the advent of computer systems of steadily advancing strength and complexity quickly rendered these systems obsolete. Such systems were not completely compliant with Kerckhoffs' Principle and still largely depended on security through obscurity in order to protect the data they processed.

To truly be able to use open cryptographic algorithms, new technologies were developed that depended on very difficult mathematical problems, sometimes referred to as one-way problems. One-way problems are generally easy to perform in one direction but very difficult to perform in the other direction. Factorization of very large numbers is an example of a one-way problem. Such problems form the basis of many modern cryptographic systems.

Symmetric versus Asymmetric Cryptography

When we look at the use of symmetric key cryptography versus asymmetric key cryptography, we do not have a situation in which one is necessarily better overall than the other for all situations. Instead, each has a set of strengths and weaknesses when used in a given situation. In many cases, symmetric key cryptography is much faster than asymmetric, but symmetric cryptography brings with it the issue of key exchange and so on. We will discuss each type of algorithm and a few specific examples of each type in this section.

SYMMETRIC CRYPTOGRAPHY

Symmetric key cryptography, also known as private key cryptography, utilizes a single key for both encryption of the plaintext and decryption of the cipher-text. The key itself must be shared between the sender and the receiver, and this process, known as key exchange, constitutes an entire subtopic of cryptography. We will discuss key exchange at greater length later in this chapter. The *symmetric* in symmetric key cryptography is a reference to the use of a single key.

One of the chief weaknesses of symmetric key cryptography lies in the use of one key. If the key is exposed beyond the sender and the receiver, it is possible for an attacker who has managed to intercept it to decrypt the message or, worse yet, to decrypt the message, alter it, then encrypt it once more and pass it on to the receiver in place of the original message. Since such issues are present, symmetric key cryptography provides only confidentiality, and not integrity, as we would not be aware that the message in our example had been altered.

Block versus Stream Ciphers

Symmetric key cryptography makes use of two types of ciphers: block ciphers and stream ciphers. A block cipher takes a predetermined number of bits, known as a block, in the plaintext message and encrypts that block. Blocks are commonly composed of 64 bits but can be larger or smaller depending on the particular algorithm being used and the various modes in which the algorithm might be capable of operating. A stream cipher encrypts each bit in the plaintext message, 1 bit at a time. It is also possible for a block cipher to act as a stream cipher by setting a block size of 1 bit.

A large majority of the encryption algorithms in use at present are block ciphers. Although block ciphers are often slower than stream ciphers, they tend to be more efficient. Since block ciphers operate on larger blocks of the message at a time, they do tend to be more resource intensive and are more complex to implement in hardware or software. Block ciphers are also more sensitive to errors in the encryption process as they are working with more data. An error in the encryption process of a block cipher may render unusable a larger segment of data than what we would find in a stream cipher, as the stream cipher would only be working with 1 particular bit.

In general, several block modes can be used with an algorithm based on a block cipher to detect and compensate for such errors. We can see such modes in use with algorithms such as the Data Encryption Standard (DES) and Advanced Encryption Standard (AES), and we will look at some of these modes in the next section when we talk about the algorithms that use them.

Typically, block ciphers are better for use in situations where the size of the message is fixed or known in advance, such as when we are encrypting a file or have message sizes that are reported in protocol headers. Stream ciphers are often better for use in situations where we have data of an unknown size or the data is in a continuous stream, such as we might see moving over a network.

Symmetric Key Algorithms

Some of the cryptographic algorithms that are more recognizable to the general public are symmetric key algorithms. Several of these, such as DES, 3DES, and AES, are or have been in regular use by the U.S. government and others as standard algorithms for protecting highly sensitive data.

DES first came into use in 1976 in the United States and has since been used by a variety of parties globally. DES is a block cipher based on symmetric key cryptography and uses a 56-bit key. Although DES was considered to be very secure for some period of time, it is no longer considered to be so. In 1999, a distributed computing project was launched to break a DES key by testing every possible key in the entire keyspace, and the project succeeded in doing so in a little more than 22 hours. This weakness brought about by the short key length was compensated for a period of time through the use of 3DES (pronounced triple DES), which is simply DES used to encrypt each block three times, each time with a different key. DES can operate in several different block modes, including Cipher Block Chaining (CBC), Electronic Code Book (ECB), Cipher Feedback (CFB), Output Feedback (OFB), and Counter Mode (CTR). Each mode changes the way encryption functions and the way errors are handled.

AES is a set of symmetric block ciphers used by the U.S. government, and now a variety of other organizations, and is the replacement for DES as the standard encryption algorithm for the U.S. federal government. AES uses three different ciphers: one with a 128-bit key, one with a 192-bit key, and one with a 256-bit key, all having a block length of 128 bits. A variety of attacks have been attempted against AES, most of them against encryption using the 128-bit key, and most of them unsuccessful, partially successful, or questionable altogether. At the time of this writing, the U.S. government still considers AES to be secure. AES shares the same block modes that DES uses and also includes other modes such as XEX-based Tweaked CodeBook (TCB) mode.

There are a large number of other well-known symmetric block ciphers, including Twofish, Serpent, Blowfish, CAST5, RC6, and IDEA, as well as stream ciphers, such as RC4, ORYX, and SEAL.

ASYMMETRIC CRYPTOGRAPHY

Although symmetric key cryptography makes use of only one key, asymmetric key cryptography, also known as public key cryptography, utilizes two keys: a public key and a private key. The public key is used to encrypt data sent from the sender to the receiver and is shared with everyone. We see public keys included in e-mail signatures, posted on servers that exist specifically to host public keys, posted on Web pages, and displayed in a number of other ways. Private keys are used to decrypt data that arrives at the receiving end and are very carefully guarded by the receiver. Complex mathematical operations are used to create the private and public keys. These operations are, at present, difficult enough that the means do not exist to reverse the private key from the public key. Asymmetric key cryptography was first described by Martin Hellman and Whitfield Diffie in their 1976 paper, "New Directions in Cryptography."[C]

[C] http://securespeech.cs.cmu.edu/reports/DiffieHellman.pdf

The main advantage of asymmetric key cryptography over symmetric key cryptography is the loss of the need to distribute the key. As we discussed earlier in this chapter, when we use a symmetric algorithm, we need to distribute the key in some way. We might do this by exchanging keys in person, sending a key in e-mail, or repeating it verbally over the phone, but we generally need to communicate the key in an out-of-band manner, meaning that we do not want to send the key with the message, as this would leave our message easily available to an eavesdropper. When we use asymmetric key cryptography, we have no need to share a single key. We simply make our public key easily available, and anyone who needs to send us an encrypted message makes use of it.

Asymmetric Key Algorithms

The RSA algorithm, named for its creators Ron Rivest, Adi Shamir, and Leonard Adleman, is an asymmetric algorithm used all over the world, including in the Secure Sockets Layer (SSL) protocol, which is used to secure many common transactions such as Web and e-mail traffic. RSA was created in 1977 and is still one of the most widely used algorithms in the world to this day.

Elliptic curve cryptography (ECC) is a class of cryptographic algorithms, although it is sometimes referred to as though it were an algorithm in and of itself. ECC is named for the type of mathematical problem on which its cryptographic functions are based. ECC has several advantages over other types of algorithms. It has a higher cryptographic strength with shorter keys than many other types of algorithms, meaning that we can use shorter keys with ECC while still maintaining a very secure form of encryption. It is also a very fast and efficient type of algorithm, allowing us to implement it on hardware with a more constrained set of resources, such as a cell phone or portable device, more easily. We can see ECC implemented in a variety of cryptographic algorithms, including Secure Hash Algorithm 2 (SHA-2) and Elliptic Curve Digital Signature Algorithm (ECDSA).

Several other asymmetric algorithms exist, including ElGamal, Diffie-Hellman, and Digital Signature Standard (DSS). We can also see a variety of protocols and applications that are based on asymmetric cryptography, including Pretty Good Privacy (PGP) for securing messages and files, SSL and Transport Layer Security (TLS) for several kinds of traffic including Web and e-mail, and some Voice over IP (VoIP) protocols for voice conversations. Asymmetric cryptography has allowed many of the modern methods of secure communication to exist and will likely continue to be the basis of them for some time.

MORE ADVANCED

PGP, created by Phil Zimmerman, was one of the first strong encryption tools to reach the eye of the general public and the media. Created in the early 1990s, the original release of PGP was based on a symmetric algorithm and could be put to use in securing data such as communications and files. The original release of PGP was given away as free software, including the source code. At the time of its release,

PGP was regulated as a munition under the U.S. International Traffic in Arms Regulations (ITAR) law. Zimmerman spent several years under investigation for criminal activities, as he was suspected of exporting PGP out of the country, which was then illegal and considered to be arms trafficking.

Hash Functions

Hash functions represent a third cryptography type alongside symmetric and asymmetric cryptography, what we might call keyless cryptography. Hash functions, also referred to as message digests, do not use a key, but instead create a largely unique and fixed-length hash value, commonly referred to as a hash, based on the original message, something along the same lines as a fingerprint.

Hashes cannot be used to discover the contents of the original message, or any of its other characteristics, but can be used to determine whether the message has changed. In this way, hashes provide confidentiality, but not integrity. Hashes are very useful when distributing files or sending communications, as the hash can be sent with the message so that the receiver can verify its integrity. The receiver simply hashes the message again using the same algorithm, then compares the two hashes. If the hashes match, the message has not changed. If they do not match, the message has been altered.

Although it is theoretically possible to engineer a matching hash for two different sets of data, called a collision, this is a very difficult task indeed, and generally requires that the hashing algorithm be broken in order to accomplish. Some algorithms, such as Message-Digest algorithm 5 (MD5), have been attacked in this fashion, although producing a collision is still nontrivial. When such cases occur, the compromised algorithm usually falls out of common use. Hashing algorithms such as SHA-2 and the soon-to-arrive SHA-3 have replaced MD5 in cases where stringent hash security is required.

Many other hash algorithms exist and are used in a variety of situations, such as MD2, MD4, and RACE.

Digital Signatures

Digital signatures are another use to which we can put asymmetric algorithms and their associated public and private keys. Digital signatures allow us to sign a message in order to enable detection of changes to the message contents, to ensure that the message was legitimately sent by the expected party, and to prevent the sender from denying that he or she sent the message, known as non-repudiation. To digitally sign a message, the sender would generate a hash of the message, and then use his private key to encrypt the hash, thus generating a digital signature. The sender would then send the digital signature along with the message, usually by appending it to the message itself.

When the message arrives at the receiving end, the receiver would use the sender's public key to decrypt the digital signature, thus restoring the original hash of the message. The receiver can then verify the integrity of the message by hashing the message again and comparing the two hashes. Although this may sound like a considerable amount of work to verify the integrity of the message, it is often done by a software application of some kind and the process typically is largely invisible to the end user.

Certificates

In addition to hashes and digital signatures, we have another construct by which we can scale up the use of message signing, in the form of digital certificates, commonly known as certificates. Certificates are created to link a public key to a particular individual and are often used as a form of electronic identification for that particular person. A certificate is typically formed by taking the public key and identifying information, such as a name and address, and having them signed by a certificate authority (CA). A CA is a trusted entity that handles digital certificates. One well-known CA, at present, is VeriSign. Additionally, some large organizations, such as the U.S. Department of Defense (DoD), that utilize a large number of certificates may choose to implement their own CA in order to keep costs down.

The advantage of having a certificate is that it allows us to verify that a public key is truly associated with a particular individual. In the case of the digital signature we discussed in the preceding section, it might be possible that someone had falsified the keys being used to sign the message and that the keys did not actually belong to the original sender. If we have a digital certificate for the sender, we can easily check with the CA to ensure that the public key for the sender is legitimate.

A CA is only a small part of the infrastructure that can be put in place to handle certificates on a large scale. This infrastructure is known as a public key infrastructure (PKI). A PKI is generally composed of two main components, although some organizations may separate some functions out into more than just these. In a PKI, we often find the CAs that issue and verify certificates and the registration authorities (RAs) that verify the identity of the individual associated with the certificate.

In PKI, we also deal with the concept of certificate revocation, in the case where a certificate reaches its expiration date, the certificate is compromised, or another reason arises in which we need to ensure that the certificate can no longer be used. In this case, we will likely see the certificate added to a certificate revocation list (CRL). The CRL is a generally public list that holds all the revoked certificates for a certain period of time, depending on the organization in question.

PROTECTING DATA AT REST, IN MOTION, AND IN USE

We can divide practical uses of cryptography into two major categories: protecting data at rest and protecting data in motion. Protecting data at rest is important because of the large amount of stored data that can be found on devices such as backup tapes, flash drives, and hard drives in portable devices such as laptops. Protecting data in motion is vital as well because of the enormous amount of business that is conducted over the Internet, including financial transactions, medical information, tax filings, and other similarly sensitive exchanges.

Protecting Data at Rest

Protecting data at rest is an area in which security is often lax and is a particularly bad area in which we choose not to emphasize security. Data is generally considered to be at rest when it is on a storage device of some kind and is not moving over a network, through a protocol, and so forth. Somewhat illogically, data at rest on media can also be in motion; for example, we might ship a load of backup tapes containing sensitive data, carry in our pocket a flash drive containing a copy of our tax forms, or leave in the back seat of our car a laptop containing the contents of a customer database.

We can see exactly this type of incident on a disturbingly regular basis in the media. In July 2010, the South Shore Hospital in South Weymouth, Massachusetts, announced that it had a breach of personal information due to the loss of backup media by a contracted data management company. The media contained sensitive information such as names, addresses, Social Security numbers, driver's license numbers, medical information, and quite a bit more on 800,000 patients [5]. Had the hospital taken the necessary steps to protect its data at rest by encrypting it, not only would it have not had such a large security incident, but it may have been spared from having to publicly disclose that the incident had occurred, thus saving the hospital quite a bit of embarrassment [6].

DATA SECURITY

A great many solutions exist for protecting data at rest. The primary method we use to protect this type of data is encryption, particularly when we know that the storage media, or the media and the device in which it is contained, will be potentially exposed to physical theft, such as on a backup tape or in a laptop.

An enormous number of commercial products are available that will provide encryption for portable devices, often focused on hard drives and portable storage devices, including products from large companies such as McAfee (presently owned by Intel), Symantec, and PGP (presently owned by Symantec), just to name a few. The features of such commercial products often include the ability to encrypt entire hard disks, known as full disk encryption, and a variety of removable media, as well as centralized management and other security and administrative features. There are also a number of free and/or open source encryption products on the market, such as TrueCrypt,[D] BitLocker,[E] which ships with some versions of Windows, dm-crypt,[F] which is specific to Linux, and many others.

[D] www.truecrypt.org/
[E] http://windows.microsoft.com/en-us/windows7/Set-up-your-hard-disk-for-BitLocker-Drive-Encryption
[F] www.saout.de/misc/dm-crypt/

We also need to be aware of the location where dataof a sensitive nature for which we are responsible is being stored and need to take appropriate measures to ensure that it is protected there.

PHYSICAL SECURITY

Physical security, which we will discuss at length in Chapter 7, is another important step in protecting data at rest. If we make it more difficult for attackers to physically access or steal the storage media on which our sensitive data is contained, we have solved a large portion of our problem. In many cases, large businesses have databases, file servers, and workstations that contain customer information, sales forecasts, business strategy documents, network diagrams, and large amounts of other data they do not wish to become public or fall into the hands of their competitors. If the physical security at the location where such data rests is weak, an attacker might be able to simply enter the building and steal a laptop, paper documentation, flash drive, or disk from a server and walk right out with the data.

> **ALERT!**
>
> Lapses in physical security are a very common starting point for security issues. If we do not take steps to ensure that our important assets are protected from a physical standpoint, we may nullify the rest of our very carefully planned security measures. Physical security should be at the core of all our security planning discussions.

We also need to be aware of the areas we cannot physically protect and need to limit the data that leaves our protected spaces. In an office building, we have a fairly limited area to protect, and we can apply even more layers of physical security to areas that might need them, such as the data center in which our servers sit. If sensitive data leaves such areas, we are very limited in what we can do to physically protect it, outside of using encryption.

We have an excellent example of a failure to protect data in both the physical and data security sense in the U.S. Department of Veterans Affairs (VA) breach that was reported in May 2010. In this case, a laptop containing unencrypted information, including Social Security numbers, on 616 veterans, was stolen from the personal vehicle of a contractor working for the VA. What makes this incident particularly unfortunate is that the VA suffered a similar breach in 2006, once again because of an unencrypted laptop stolen from a personal vehicle. In this case, the breach was much more severe because the set of data lost related to 28.5 million veterans and service members, ultimately costing the VA $48 million to clean up [7]. In the words of George Santayana, "Those who cannot remember the past are doomed to repeat it" [8].

Protecting Data in Motion

Another major concern to protecting our data comes when it is in motion over a network of some variety. This might be over a closed WAN or LAN, over a wireless network, over the Internet, or in other ways. The primary method of securing data from exposure on network media is encryption, and we may choose to apply it in one of two main ways: by encrypting the data itself to protect it, or by protecting the entire connection.

PROTECTING THE DATA ITSELF

We can take a variety of approaches to protect the data we are sending over the network, depending on what data we are sending and the protocols over which we are sending it.

SSL and TLS are often used to protect information sent over networks and over the Internet, and they operate in conjunction with other protocols such as Internet Message Access Protocol (IMAP) and Post Office Protocol (POP) for e-mail, Hypertext Transfer Protocol (HTTP) for Web traffic, VoIP for voice conversations, instant messaging, and hundreds of others. SSL is actually the predecessor of TLS, and TLS is based heavily on the last version of SSL. The terms are often used interchangeably, and they are nearly identical to each other. Both methods are still in common use.

When SSL/TLS is used, it encrypts a connection between two systems communicating over a network but is generally specific to a particular application or protocol. So, although we might be using SSL/TLS to encrypt our communications with the server that holds our e-mail, this does not necessarily mean the connections made through our Web browser enjoy the same level of increased security. Many common applications are capable of supporting SSL/TLS, but they generally need to be configured to do so independently.

PROTECTING THE CONNECTION

Another approach we might choose to take is to encrypt all our network traffic with a virtual private network (VPN) connection. VPN connections use a variety of protocols to make a secure connection between two systems. We might use a VPN when we are connecting from a potentially insecure network, such as the wireless connection in a hotel, to the internal resources that are secure behind our company firewalls.

Although a variety of protocols can be used to secure a VPN connection, and many have been developed and used over the years, two main methods are used at present: Internet Protocol Security (IPsec) VPNs and SSL VPNs. These two types of VPN connections can be configured to a nearly identical set of features and functionality, from the perspective of the user, but they require a slightly different set of hardware and software to set up. Typically, an IPsec VPN requires a more complex hardware configuration on the back end and a software client to be installed, whereas an SSL VPN often operates from a lightweight plug-in downloaded from a Web page and a less complex hardware configuration on the back end. From a security footing standpoint, the two methods are relatively equivalent in terms of encryption. It is possible that the SSL VPN client might be downloaded to a public computer or other random computer, due to its ease of installation, and provide an avenue for data leakage or attack because of the potentially insecure state of the system.

Protecting Data in Use

The last category of protecting data involves securing it while it is being used. Although we can use encryption to protect data while it is stored or moving across a network, we are somewhat limited in our ability to protect data while it is being used by those who legitimately have access to it. Authorized users can print files, move them to other machines or storage devices, e-mail them, share them on peer-to-peer (P2P) file-sharing networks, and generally make a mockery of our carefully laid security measures.

In 2009, it was discovered that classified information containing details on the communications, navigation, and management electronics systems for Marine One, the helicopter used to transport the president of the United States, had been leaked onto a P2P network from the computer of a government contractor. A copy of the data was also found to have been shared from a machine with an Iranian IP address [9]. Clearly, this is a case of extremely sensitive data being lost while in use, but we can also see many examples of companies that hold and work with data sensitive to businesses and individuals on a regular basis.

CRYPTOGRAPHY IN THE REAL WORLD

As we mentioned a few times in this chapter, cryptography is one of the main tools that have allowed us to become a very network-centric society. We buy items online, play games over the Internet, send and receive e-mail, surf the Web, use social networking tools such as Twitter and Facebook through a variety of interfaces and devices, and connect to wireless networks, and we do almost all of this in a secure fashion through the use of cryptography.

A few main protocols secure much of this traffic for us. SSL/TLS encrypts quite a bit of our network traffic including e-mail, Web browsing, VoIP, and others. SSL/TLS can use a variety of algorithms, including AES. When we use VPNs to encrypt entire connections, we generally see either IPsec or SSL used to encrypt the VPN connection. IPsec can again use a variety of algorithms. Depending on how exactly it is configured, we might find AES, MD5, SHA-1, 3DES, or even DES in use.

To secure communications between two machines, we might see the Secure Shell (SSH) protocol in use, typically on port 22. The utilities that allow us to use SSH are generally installed by default on Linux- and UNIX-based systems, and are supported on most other operating systems as well. SSH is such a widely used tool that support for most any cryptographic algorithm can be found in one implementation or another, including 3DES, Blowfish, AES, Serpent, and IDEA, just to name a few [10]. SSH can provide security for terminal connections, file transfers, remote desktop tools, VPN connectivity, Web browsing, and most any other application to which we might care to apply it.

Kerberos is a somewhat complex network authentication protocol, the intimate details of which are beyond the scope of our discussion here, but it is nonetheless worthy of mention, as it is commonly used. Kerberos provides the basis of many single sign-on (SSO) implementations. SSO allows us to create a set of associated applications or systems that can all be accessed through a centralized login system. Kerberos also serves as the basis for Microsoft's Active Directory. As with many of the other cryptographic applications we have discussed, Kerberos can make use of a variety of cryptographic protocols.

SUMMARY

Cryptography has existed, in one form or another, for most of recorded history. We can see examples of such practices that stretch in complexity from very simple substitution ciphers, to the fairly complex electromechanical machines that were used just before the invention of the first modern computing systems. Although such primitive cryptographic methods would not stand up under modern methods of cryptographic attacks, they still form the basis for our modern algorithms.

There are three main categories of cryptographic algorithms: symmetric key cryptography, also known as private key cryptography; asymmetric key cryptography, also known as public key cryptography; and hash functions that we might refer to as keyless cryptography. In private key cryptography, the key is used for both encryption and decryption and is shared by all parties that need to operate on the plaintext or ciphertext. In public key cryptography, we use a public and a private key. The sender encrypts the message with the receiver's public key, and the receiver decrypts the message with their private key. This resolves the problem of having to find a secure way to share a single private key between the receiver and the sender. Hash functions do not use a key at all but are used to create a theoretically unique fingerprint of the message so that we can tell if the message has been altered from its original form.

Digital signatures are an extension of hash functions that allow us to not only create a hash to ensure that the message has not been altered but also encrypt the hash with the public key of an asymmetric algorithm to ensure that the message was sent by the expected party and to provide for nonrepudiation.

Certificates allow us to link a public key to a particular identity so that we can ensure that an encrypted message really represents a communication from a particular individual. The receiver can check with the issuer of the certificate, the CA, in order to determine whether the certificate presented is, in fact, legitimate. Behind the CA, we may find a PKI, which supports the issuing, verification, and revocation of certificates.

In general, cryptography provides us with a mechanism to protect data at rest, in motion, and, to a certain extent, in use. It provides the core of many of the basic security mechanisms that enable us to communicate and carry out transactions when the data involved is of a sensitive nature and we would prefer that it not be exposed to the general public or to attackers.

EXERCISES

1. What type of cipher is a Caesar cipher?
2. What is the difference between a block and a stream cipher?
3. ECC is classified as which type of cryptographic algorithm?
4. What is the key point of Kerckhoffs' Principle?
5. What is a substitution cipher?
6. What are the main differences between symmetric and asymmetric key cryptography?
7. Explain how 3DES differs from DES.
8. How does public key cryptography work?
9. Decrypt this message: V qb abg srne pbzchgref. V srne gur ynpx bs gurz. -Vfnnp Nfvzbi
10. How is physical security important when discussing cryptographic security of data?

Bibliography

[1] U.S. National Security Agency, Enigma machine, U.S. National Security Agency. <www.nsa.gov/about/_images/pg_hi_res/enigma_machine.jpg>, 2010.

[2] U.S. National Security Agency, Photo Gallery. About NSA, U.S. National Security Agency. <www.nsa.gov/about/photo_gallery/gallery.shtml>, January 15, 2009 (accessed: January 3, 2011).

[3] F. Petitcolas, "la cryptographie militaire," petitcolas.net. <http://petitcolas.net/fabien/kerckhoffs/#english>, March 14, 2010 (accessed: January 3, 2011).

[4] J. Jacobs, The enemy knows the system, and the allies do not, ISSA J. (2010).

[5] S. Scheible, South Shore Hospital says 800,000 patient records missing, The Patriot Ledger. <www.patriotledger.com/homepage/breaking/x999357727/South-Shore-Hospital-says-patient-records-may-be-lost-by-outside-data-firm>, July 19, 2010 (accessed: January 10, 2011).

[6] U.S. Department of Health and Human Services, HITECH Breach Notification Interim Final Rule, HHS.gov. <www.hhs.gov/ocr/privacy/hipaa/understanding/coveredentities/breachnotificationifr.html>, 2011 (accessed: January 10, 2011).

[7] J.N. Hoover, Stolen VA laptop contains personal data, Information Week Government. <www.informationweek.com/news/government/security/showArticle.jhtml?articleID=224800060>, May 14, 2010 (accessed: January 10, 2011).

[8] G. Santayana, Reason in Common Sense: The Life of Reason, vol. 1, Dover Publications, 1980. EAN: 978-0486239194.

[9] J. Vijayan, Classified data on president's helicopter leaked via P2P, found on Iranian computer, Computerworld. <www.computerworld.com/s/article/9128820/Classified_data_on_president_s_helicopter_leaked_via_P2P_found_on_Iranian_computer>, March 2, 2009 (accessed: January 11, 2011).

[10] T. Ylonen, C. Lonvick, RFC 4253. IETF.org. <www.ietf.org/rfc/rfc4253.txt>, January 2006 (accessed: January 17, 2011).

CHAPTER 6

Operations Security

Information in This Chapter:

- Origins of Operations Security
- The Operations Security Process
- Laws of Operations Security
- Operations Security in Our Personal Lives

INTRODUCTION

Operations security, known in military and government circles as OPSEC, is, at a high level, a process that we use to protect our information. Although we have discussed certain elements of operations security previously, such as the use of encryption to protect data, such measures are only a small portion of the entire operations security process.

> **ALERT!**
>
> Although the formal methodology of operations security is generally considered to be a governmental or military concept, the ideas that it represents are useful not only in this setting but also in the conduct of business and in our personal lives. Throughout the chapter, when we discuss the specific government use of operations security, we will refer to it as OPSEC, and outside of that specific use as operations security, in order to differentiate between the general concept and the specific methodology.

The entire process involves not only putting countermeasures in place, but before doing so, carefully identifying what exactly we need to protect, and what we need to protect it against. If we jump directly to putting protective measures in place, we have put the cart before the horse and might not be directing our efforts toward the information assets that are actually the most critical items to protect. It is important to remember when putting security measures in place that we should be implementing security measures that are relative to the value of what we are protecting. If we evenly apply the same level of security to everything, we may be overprotecting some things that are not of high value and underprotecting things of much greater value.

ORIGINS OF OPERATIONS SECURITY

Operations security may be a fairly recent idea, as far as the specific implementation of OPSEC by the U.S. government is concerned, but the concepts comprising it are truly ancient indeed. We can see such ideas put forth in the works of Sun Tzu thousands of years ago, and in the words of the founders of the United States, such as George Washington and Benjamin Franklin. While we can point to nearly any period in history, and nearly any military or large commercial organization, and find the principles of operations security present, a few specific occasions present themselves as being particularly influential in the development and use of operations security.

Sun Tzu

Sun Tzu was a Chinese military general who lived in the sixth century BC. Among those of a military or strategic bent, Sun Tzu's work *The Art of War* is considered to be somewhat of a bible for conducting such operations. *The Art of War* has spawned countless clones and texts that apply the principles it espouses to a variety of situations, including, but not limited to, information security. The text provides some of the earliest examples of operations security principles that are plainly stated and clearly documented.

We can point out numerous passages within *The Art of War* as being related to operations security principles. We will look at just a couple of them for the sake of brevity.

The first passage is "If I am able to determine the enemy's dispositions while at the same time I conceal my own, then I can concentrate and he must divide" [1]. This is a simple admonition to discover information held by our opponents while protecting our own. This is one of the most basic tenets of operations security.

ADDITIONAL RESOURCES

The Art of War is a great resource for those who are involved in information security and is definitely a recommended read. A paper copy can be found at most any good bookstore, and an online version is available for free on the Project Gutenberg Web site, www.gutenberg.org/ebooks/132.

The second passage is "(when) making tactical dispositions, the highest pitch you can attain is to conceal them; conceal your dispositions, and you will be safe from prying of the subtlest spies, from the machinations of the wisest brains" [1]. Here, Sun Tzu is saying we should conduct our strategic planning in an area that is very difficult for our opponents to observe, specifically the highest point we can find. Again, this is a recommendation to very carefully protect our planning activities so that they do not leak to those that might oppose our efforts. For having been penned such a long time ago, the writings of Sun Tzu, as they relate to operations security, are still applicable to this day.

George Washington

George Washington, the first president of the United States, was well known for being an astute and skilled military commander and is also well known for promoting good operational security practices. He is known in the operations security community for having said, "Even minutiae should have a place in our collection, for things of a seemingly trifling nature, when enjoined with others of a more serious cast, may lead to valuable conclusion" [2], meaning that even small items of information, which are valueless individually, can be of great value in combination. We can see an example of exactly this in the three main items of information that constitute an identity: a name, an address, and a Social Security number. Individually, these items are completely useless. We could take any one of them in isolation and put it up on a billboard for the world to see, and not be any worse for having done so. In combination, these three items are sufficient for an attacker to steal our identity and use it for all manners of fraudulent activities.

Washington is also quoted as having said, "For upon Secrecy, Success depends in most Enterprizes of the kind, and for want of it, they are generally defeated" [3]. In this case, he was referring to an intelligence gathering program and the particular need to keep its activities secret. He is often considered to have been very well informed on intelligence issues and is credited with maintaining a fairly extensive organization to execute such activities, long before any such formal capabilities existed in the United States.

Vietnam War

During the Vietnam War, the United States came to realize that information regarding troop movements, operations, and other military activities was being leaked to the enemy. Clearly, in most environments, military or otherwise, having our opponents gain foreknowledge of our activities is a bad thing, particularly so when lives may be at stake. In an effort to curtail this unauthorized passing of information, a study, codenamed Purple Dragon, a symbol of OPSEC that persists to this day, as shown in Figure 6.1, was conducted to crack down the cause.

Ultimately, the study brought about two main ideas: first, in that particular environment, eavesdroppers and spies abounded; and second, a survey was needed to get to the bottom of the information loss. The survey asked questions about the information itself, vulnerability analysis, and other items. The team conducting these surveys and analyses also coined the term *operations*

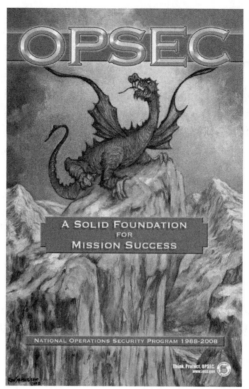

FIGURE 6.1
OPSEC Purple Dragon Poster

security and the acronym *OPSEC*. Additionally, they saw the need for an operations security group to serve as a body that would espouse the principles of operations security to the different organizations within the government and work with them to get them established, but this was not to happen yet.

Business

In the late 1970s and early 1980s, some of the operations security concepts that were used in the world of the military and government were beginning to take root in the commercial world. The ideas of industrial espionage and spying on our business competition in order to gain a competitive advantage have been around since the beginning of time, but as such concepts were becoming more structured in the military world, they were becoming more structured in the business world as well. In 1980, Michael Porter, a professor at Harvard Business School, published a book titled *Competitive Strategy: Techniques for Analyzing Industries and Competitors*. This text, now nearing its sixtieth printing, set the basis for what is referred to as competitive intelligence.

Competitive intelligence is generally defined as the process of intelligence gathering and analysis in order to support business decisions. The counterpart of competitive intelligence, competitive counterintelligence, correlates in a fairly direct manner to the operations security principles that were laid out by the government only a few years previously, and is an active part of conducting business to this day. We can see these principles at work in many large corporations, as well as in groups such as the Strategic and Competitive Intelligence Professionals (SCIP)[A] professional organization and the Ecole de Guerre Economique, or Economic Warfare School, located in Paris.

Interagency OPSEC Support Staff

After the end of the Vietnam War, the group that conducted Purple Dragon and developed the government OPSEC principles tried to get support for an interagency group that would work with the various government agencies on operations security. Unfortunately, they had little success in interesting the various military institutions and were unable to gain official support from the U.S. National Security Agency (NSA). Fortunately, through the efforts of the U.S. Department of Energy (DOE) and the U.S. General Services Administration (GSA), they were able to gain sufficient backing to move forward. At this point, a document was drafted to put in front of then-first-term-President Ronald Reagan.

These efforts were delayed due to Reagan's reelection campaign, but shortly afterward, in 1988, the Interagency OPSEC Support Staff (IOSS) was signed into being with the National Decision Security Directive 298 [4]. The IOSS is responsible for a wide variety of OPSEC awareness and training efforts, such as the poster shown in Figure 6.2.

THE OPERATIONS SECURITY PROCESS

The operations security process, as laid out by the U.S. government, will look very familiar to anyone who has worked with risk management. In essence, the process is to identify what information we have that needs protection, analyze the threats and vulnerabilities that might impact it, and develop methods of mitigation for those threats and vulnerabilities, as shown in Figure 6.3.

Although the process is relatively simple, it is very effective and time tested.

Identification of Critical Information

The initial step, and, arguably, the most important step in the operations security process, is to identify our most critical information assets. Although we could spend a great deal of time identifying every little item of information that might even remotely be of importance, this is not the goal in this step of the operations security process. For any given business, individual, military operation, process, or project, there are bound to be at least a few critical items of information on which everything else depends. For a soft drink company it might be our secret recipe, for an application vendor it might be our

---

[A]www.scip.org/

FIGURE 6.2
OPSEC Awareness Poster

source code, for a military operation it might be our attack timetable, and so on. These are the assets that most need protection and will cause us the most harm if exposed, and these are the assets we should be identifying.

Analysis of Threats

As we discussed in Chapter 1 when we covered threats, vulnerabilities, and risks, a threat is something that has the potential to cause us harm. In the case of analyzing threats to our information assets, we would start with the critical information we identified in the previous step. With the list of critical information, we can then begin to look at what harm might be caused by critical information being exposed, and who might exploit the exposure. This is the same process used by many military and government organizations to classify information and determine who is allowed to see it.

For instance, if we are a software company that has identified the proprietary source code of one of our main products as an item of critical information, we might determine that the chief threats of such an exposure could be exposure to attackers and exposure to our competition. If the source code were exposed to attackers, they might be able to determine the scheme we use to generate

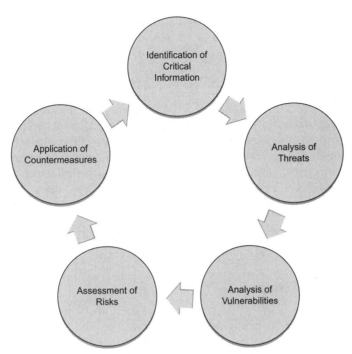

FIGURE 6.3
Operations Security Process

license keys for our products in order to prevent piracy, and use access to the source code to develop a utility that could generate legitimate keys, thus costing us revenue to software piracy. In the case of our competition, they might use access to our source code to copy features for use in their own applications, or they might copy large portions of our application and sell it themselves.

This step in the process needs to be repeated for each item of information we have identified as being critical, for each party that might take advantage of it if it were exposed, and for each use they might make of the information. Logically, the more information assets we identify as being critical, the more involved this step becomes. In some circumstances, we may find that only a limited number of parties are capable of making use of the information, and then only in a limited number of ways, and in some cases we may find the exact opposite. This type of analysis is highly situational.

Analysis of Vulnerabilities

As with our discussion on threats, we also talked about vulnerabilities in Chapter 1. Vulnerabilities are weaknesses that can be used to harm us. In the case of analyzing the vulnerabilities in the protections we have put in place for our information assets, we will be looking at how the processes that interact with these assets are normally conducted, and where we might attack in order to compromise them. When we looked at threats, we used the source code of a software company as an example of an item of critical information that might cause us harm if it were to find its way into the hands of our competition.

When we look at vulnerabilities, we might find that our security controls on the source code with which we are concerned are not very rigorous, and that it is possible to access, copy, delete, or alter it without any authorization beyond that needed to access the operating system or network shares. This might make it possible for an attacker who has compromised the system to copy, tamper with, or entirely delete the source code, or might render the files vulnerable to accidental alteration while the system is undergoing maintenance. We might also find there are no policies in place that regulate how the source code is handled, in the sense of where it should be stored, whether copies of it should exist on other systems or on backup media, and how it should be protected in general. These issues, in combination, might present multiple vulnerabilities that could have the potential to lead to serious breaches of our security.

Assessment of Risks

Assessment of risks is where the proverbial rubber meets the road, in terms of deciding what issues we really need to be concerned about during the operations security process. As we discussed in Chapter 1, risk occurs when we have a matching threat and vulnerability, and only then. To go back to our software source code example, we had determined that we had seen a threat in the potential for our application source code being exposed in an unauthorized manner. Furthermore, we found that we had a threat in the poor controls on access to our source code, and a lack of policy in how exactly it was controlled. These two matching issues could potentially lead to the exposure of our critical information to our competitors or attackers.

It is important to note again that we need a matching threat and vulnerability to constitute a risk. If the confidentiality of our source code was not an issue— for instance, if we were creating an open source project and the source code was freely available to the public—we would not have a risk in this particular case. Likewise, if our source code were subject to very stringent security requirements that would make it a near impossibility for it to be released in an unauthorized manner, we would also not have a risk.

Application of Countermeasures

Once we have discovered what risks to our critical information might be present, we would then put measures in place to mitigate them. Such measures are referred to in operations security as countermeasures. As we discussed, in order to constitute a risk, we need a matching set of threats and vulnerabilities. When we construct a countermeasure for a particular risk, in order to do the bare minimum, we need only to mitigate either the threat or the vulnerability. In the case of our source code example, the threat was that our source code might be exposed to our competitors or attackers, and the vulnerability was the poor set of security controls we had in place to protect it. In this instance, there is not much that we can do to protect ourselves from the threat itself without changing the nature of our application entirely, so there is really not a good step for us to take to mitigate the threat. We can, however, put measures in place to mitigate the vulnerability.

In the case of our source code example, we had a vulnerability to match the threat because of the poor controls on the handling of the code itself. If we institute stronger measures on controlling access to the code and also put policy in place to lay out a set of rules for how it is to be handled, we will largely remove this vulnerability. Once we have broken the threat/vulnerability pair, we will likely no longer be left with much in the way of a serious risk.

It is important to note that this is an iterative process; once we reach the end of the cycle, we will, in all likelihood, need to go through the cycle more than once in order to fully mitigate any issues. Each time we go through the cycle, we will do so based on the knowledge and experience we gained from our previous mitigation efforts, and we will be able to tune our solution for an even greater level of security. In addition, when our environment changes and new factors arise, we will need to revisit this process.

For those familiar with the risk management process, we might notice a missing step from the operations security side when comparing the two processes, namely, an evaluation of the effectiveness of our countermeasures. It is the author's belief that this is implied in the operations security process. However, the process is certainly not set in stone and there is absolutely no reason not to formally include this step if it is desired. In fact, we may see great benefit from doing so.

LAWS OF OPERATIONS SECURITY

As a somewhat different, and briefer, viewpoint on the operations security process, we can look at the Laws of OPSEC, developed by Kurt Haas while he was employed at the Nevada Operations Office of the DOE. These laws represent a distillation of the operations security process we discussed earlier and, while we might not necessarily call them the most important parts of the process, they do serve to highlight some of the main concepts of the overall procedure.

First Law

The first law of operations security is "If you don't know the threat, how do you know what to protect?" [5]. This law refers to the need to develop an awareness of both the actual and potential threats that our critical data might face. This law maps directly to the second step in the operations security process.

Ultimately, as we discussed earlier, we may face many threats against our critical information. Each item of information may have a unique set of threats and may have multiple threats, each from a different source. Particularly as we see the surge of services that are cloud based, it is also important to understand that threats may be location dependent. We may have enumerated all the threats that face our critical data for a particular location, but if we have our data replicated across multiple storage areas in multiple countries due to a cloud-based storage mechanism, threats may differ from one storage location to another. Different parties may have better or easier potential access in one particular area, or the laws may differ significantly from one location to another and pose entirely new threats.

MORE ADVANCED

Cloud computing refers to services that are hosted, often over the Internet, for the purposes of delivering easily scaled computing services or resources. Cloud-based services often use a hardware and network infrastructure that is spread over many devices in a widely distributed fashion, often spanning geographic borders. We can see examples of cloud-based offerings from many companies at present, including Google, Microsoft, IBM, and Amazon, just to name a few. The security of cloud services and the data they contain is very much a hot topic in the information security world at present and will likely continue to be for some period of time. Depending on the data and services we are considering hosting in an environment that is largely out of our direct control, the risk may be considerable.

Not only is it important to understand the threats and sources of threats themselves, but it is also important to understand the repercussions of exposure in a specific situation so that we can plan our countermeasures for that particular occurrence very specifically.

Second Law

"If you don't know what to protect, how do you know you are protecting it?" [5]. This law of operations security discusses the need to evaluate our information assets and determine what exactly we might consider to be our critical information. This second law equates to the first step in the operations security process.

In the vast majority of government environments, identification and classification of information is mandated. Each item of information, perhaps a document or file, is assigned a label that attests to the sensitivity of its contents, such as classified, top secret, and so forth. Such labeling makes the task of identifying our critical information considerably easier, but is, unfortunately, not as frequently used outside of government. In the business world, we may see the policy that dictates the use of such information classification, but, in the experience of the author, such labeling is usually implemented sporadically, at best. A few civilian industries, such as those that deal with data that has federally mandated requirements for protection (financial data, medical data), do utilize information classification, but these are the exception rather than the rule.

Third Law

The third and last law of operations security is "If you are not protecting it (the information), … THE DRAGON WINS!" [5]. This law is an overall reference to the necessity of the operations security process. If we do not take steps to protect our information from the dragon (our adversaries or competitors), they win by default.

The case of the "dragon" winning—from the constant appearance of security breaches reported by the news media and on Web sites that track breaches, such as www.datalossdb.org—appears to be unfortunately common. In many cases, we can examine a breach and find that it was the result of simple carelessness and noncompliance with the most basic security measures and due diligence. We can see an example of exactly this in a breach announced by Louisiana's Tulane University in January 2011.

In this case, the university exposed a database containing the names, addresses, Social Security numbers, and tax documents for every employee of the school, more than 10,000 individuals all told [6]. Although we might assume that a wily band of hackers had subverted the university's stringent security measures and managed to steal a copy of the database from a protected system on the university network, this is sadly not the case. The employee data was located on an unencrypted laptop, which was placed in a briefcase and left in a car by a university employee that had gone out of town.

In such cases, the operations security process, when properly followed, will quickly point out critical data sets such as these, enabling us to stand a much better chance of avoiding such a situation. The security measures needed to prevent breaches such as those we discussed in the Tulane example are neither complex nor expensive and can save us a great deal of reputational and financial damage by taking the few steps needed to put them in place.

OPERATIONS SECURITY IN OUR PERSONAL LIVES

Although we have discussed the use of the operations security process in both business and government throughout this chapter, it can also be of great use in our personal lives. Although we might not consciously and formally step through all the steps of the operations security process to protect our personal data, we still do use some of the methods we have discussed.

f we will be going on vacation for several weeks and will be leav-
empty house for the whole time, the steps we take to ensure
security while we are gone will generally map very closely to
security process. We might take a few minutes to think about the
the house is unoccupied and vulnerable:

n at night
oming from the house when we would normally be home
s building up in the driveway

- Mail building up in the mailbox
- No car in the driveway
- No people coming and going

We might also take steps to ensure that we do not present such an obvious display of vulnerabilities to those that might threaten the security of our domicile, namely burglars or vandals. We might set timers on our lights so that they turn on and off at various times throughout the house. We may also set a timer on the television or radio so that we can generate noise consistent with someone being home. In order to solve the problem of mail and newspapers stacking up, we can have the delivery of them suspended while we are gone. To give the appearance of occupation, we might also have a friend drop by every few days to water the plants and check on things, perhaps moving a car in and out of the garage every now and then.

ALERT!

In the age of social networking tools, one particular personal operations security violation can be seen on a disturbingly regular basis. Many such tools are now equipped with location awareness functionality that can allow our computers and portable devices to report our physical location when we update our status. Additionally, many people are fond of adding notifications that they are going to lunch, leaving on vacation, and so on. In both of these instances, we have left the general public, and potentially, attackers, a very clear signal of when we might not be home, when we might be found at a particular location, and so forth. From an operational security standpoint, this is ill advised.

Although such steps are clearly not strictly regimented and militaristic in nature, such as we might find with OPSEC being implemented by the government, the process is the same. Most of us follow such processes when we protect our physical property due to the obvious nature of the threat, but we also need to take care to protect ourselves in the logical sense.

In our daily lives, our personal information goes through a staggering variety of computer systems and over a large number of networks. Although we might take steps to ensure that we mitigate security threats by being careful about where and how we share our personal information over the Internet, shredding mail that contains sensitive information before throwing it away, and other similar measures, we are, unfortunately, not in control of all the places our personal information might be exposed.

As we pointed out with the Tulane breach example earlier in this chapter, not everyone will take the same care with our information. In such cases, if we have planned for the security of our personal data in advance, we can at least mitigate the issue to a certain extent. We can put monitoring services in place to watch our reports with the credit reporting agencies, we can file fraud reports with these same agencies in the case of a breach, we can very carefully watch our financial accounts, and other similar measures. Although such steps might not be complex, or terribly difficult to carry out, they are better done in advance of an incident, rather than trying to carry them out in the chaotic time directly after the problem has occurred.

OPERATIONS SECURITY IN THE REAL WORLD

As we have discussed throughout the chapter, we can see the concepts of operations security at work in many areas. In government, we can see the formalized use of OPSEC as a mandate. Clearly, when we are dealing with information pertaining to conducting wars and military actions, weapons systems of great power, political maneuvering, and other similar activities, protecting such items of information is critical and may result in the loss of many lives if we fail to do so.

In the business world, we may see the same operations security principles at work, but we may also see a large amount of variance in the way they are implemented. Depending on the industry in which we are conducting business and the types of information we are handling, we may see more or less of an operations security focus. In some cases, such as when our business is handling medical, financial, or educational information, for instance, we may fall under regulatory or contractual controls that require us to put certain protections in place. In these instances, we are much more likely to see the concepts of operations security applied with some level of rigidity. Otherwise, businesses may or may not choose to apply such ideas as they see fit.

In our personal lives, we may also choose to apply the principles of operations security, although often in a much more informal manner. Although we may not necessarily have nuclear secrets or databases full of personal information to protect, we still have quite a few items that might be considered critical information. We need to protect our financial information, data concerning our identity, personal records, or other items we might not want to be made public. In such cases, we may often shortcut the operations security process to simply identifying and finding ways to protect our personal information, but we are still going through the same general steps.

SUMMARY

The history of operational security stretches far back into recorded history. We can find such principles espoused in the writings of Sun Tzu in the sixth century BC, in the words of George Washington, in writings from the business community, and in formal methodologies from the U.S. government. Although the formalized ideas of operations security are a much more recent creation, the principles on which they are founded are ancient indeed.

The operations security process consists of five major steps. We start by identifying our most critical information so that we know what we need to protect. We then analyze our situation in order to determine what threats we might face, and following that what vulnerabilities exist in our environment. Once we know what threats and vulnerabilities we face, we can attempt to determine what risks we might face. The actual risks that are present are a combination of matching threats and vulnerabilities. When we know what risks we face, we can then plan out the countermeasures we might put in place in order to mitigate our risks.

As somewhat of a summarization of the operations security process, we can also look to the Laws of OPSEC, as penned by Kurt Haas. "If you don't know the threat, how do you know what to protect?" "If you don't know what to protect, how do you know you are protecting it?" "If you are not protecting it (the information), … THE DRAGON WINS!" [5]. These three laws cover some of the high points of the process and point out some of the more important aspects we might want to internalize.

In addition to the use of the operations security principles in business and in government, we also make use of such security concepts in our personal lives, even though we may not do so in a formal manner. We often take the steps of identifying our critical information and planning out measures to protect it in the normal course of our lives. Particularly with the sheer volume of our personal information that moves through a variety of systems and networks, it becomes increasingly important for us to take steps to protect it.

EXERCISES

1. Why is it important to identify our critical information?
2. What is the first law of OPSEC?
3. What is the function of the IOSS?
4. What part did George Washington play in the origination of operations security?
5. In the operations security process, what is the difference between assessing threats and assessing vulnerabilities?
6. Why might we want to use information classification?
7. When we have cycled through the entire operations security process, are we finished?
8. From where did the first formal OPSEC methodology arise?
9. What is the origin of operations security?
10. Define competitive counterintelligence.

Bibliography

[1] S. Tzu, S.B. Griffith, B.H. Liddell Hart, The Art of War, Oxford University Press, 1971. ISBN-13: 9780195014761.

[2] The Operations Security Professional's Association, The Origin of OPSEC, The Operations Security Professional's Association. <www.opsecprofessionals.org/origin.html>, 2011 (accessed: February 21, 2011).

[3] U.S. Central Intelligence Agency, George Washington, 1789–97, U.S. Central Intelligence Agency, <https://www.cia.gov/library/center-for-the-study-of-intelligence/csi-publications/books-and-monographs/our-first-line-of-defense-presidential-reflections-on-us-intelligence/washington.html>, July 7, 2008 (accessed: January 18, 2011).

[4] The White House, National Security Decision Directive Number 298, The White House, 1988.

[5] K. Haas, Kurt's Laws of OPSEC, vol. II, National Classification Management Society, 1992. ISSN-0009-8434.

[6] wwltv.com, Tulane: Laptop stolen with W-2 info, S.S. numbers of each employee, WWLTV.com. <www.wwltv.com/news/Tulane-Laptop-stolen-with-SS-numbers-of-every-employees-113115159. html>, January 7, 2011 (accessed: January 23, 2011).

CHAPTER 7
Physical Security

Information in This Chapter:
- Physical Security Controls
- Protecting People
- Protecting Data
- Protecting Equipment

INTRODUCTION

Physical security is largely concerned with the protection of three main categories of assets: people, equipment, and data. Our primary concern, of course, is to protect people. People are considerably more difficult to replace than equipment or data, particularly when they are experienced in their particular field and are familiar with the processes and tasks they perform.

Next in order of priority of protection is our data. If we have sufficiently planned and prepared in advance, we should be able to easily protect our data from any disaster that is not global in scale. If we do not prepare for such an issue, we can very easily lose our data permanently.

> **ALERT!**
>
> Although we will discuss the protection of people, data, and equipment as separate concepts in this chapter, they are actually closely integrated. We generally cannot, and should not, develop security plans that protect any of these categories in isolation from the others.

Lastly, we protect our equipment and the facilities that house it. This may seem to be a very important set of objects to which we might want to assign a greater level of priority when planning our physical security measures. However, this is generally not the case, outside of a few situations, most of which actually revolve around keeping people safe. In the technology world, much of the hardware we use is relatively generic and easily replaced. Even if we are using more specialized equipment, we can often replace it in a matter of days or weeks.

In many larger organizations, protection of people, data, and equipment is covered under a set of policies and procedures collectively referred to as business continuity planning and disaster recovery planning, often simply called BCP/DRP. BCP refers specifically to the plans we put in place to ensure that critical business functions can continue in a state of emergency. DRP covers the plans we put in place in preparation for a potential disaster, and what exactly we will do during and after a particular disaster strikes.

The threats we face when we are concerned with physical security generally fall into a few main categories, as listed here and shown in Figure 7.1:

- Extreme temperature
- Gases
- Liquids
- Living organisms
- Projectiles
- Movement
- Energy anomalies
- People
- Toxins
- Smoke and fire

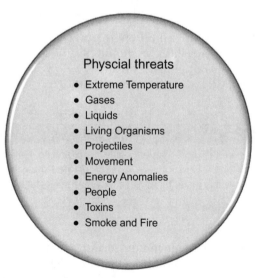

Physcial threats
- Extreme Temperature
- Gases
- Liquids
- Living Organisms
- Projectiles
- Movement
- Energy Anomalies
- People
- Toxins
- Smoke and Fire

FIGURE 7.1
Major Categories of Physical Threats

The first seven of these categories—extreme temperature, gases, liquids, living organisms, projectiles, movement, and energy anomalies—were defined by Donn Parker in his book *Fighting Computer Crime*.

ADDITIONAL RESOURCES

The book *Fighting Computer Crime*, also the source of the Parkerian hexad that we discussed in Chapter 1, is a must-read for the serious information security practitioner. Although it was written more than a decade ago, it is still very relevant to the field and is an excellent book as well. It is available from Wiley (ISBN: 0471163783).

As we move through the sections in this chapter on protecting people, equipment, and data, we will discuss how the different threats apply to each of them. In some cases, we might find that all the threats apply in a given category, or we may find that some of them are nullified entirely.

PHYSICAL SECURITY CONTROLS

Physical security controls are the devices, systems, people, and other methods we put in place to ensure our security in a physical sense. There are three main types of physical controls: deterrent, detective, and preventive, as shown in Figure 7.2. Each has a different focus, but none is completely distinct and separate from the others, as we will discuss shortly. Additionally, these controls work best when used in concert. Any one of them is not sufficient to ensure our physical security in most situations.

Deterrent

Deterrent controls are designed to discourage those who might seek to violate our security controls from doing so. A variety of controls might be considered

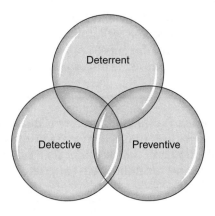

FIGURE 7.2
Types of Security Controls

to be a deterrent, including, as we discussed earlier in this section, several that overlap with the other categories. In the sense of pure detective controls, we can point to specific items that are intended to indicate that other controls may be in place.

Examples of this include signs in public places that indicate that video monitoring is in place, and the yard signs with alarm company logos that we might find in residential areas. The signs themselves do nothing to prevent people from acting in an undesirable fashion, but they do point out that there may be consequences for doing so. Such measures, while not directly adding to what we might think of as physical security, do help to keep honest people honest.

We may also see security measures in the other categories serve double duty as deterrents. If we have obvious security measures in place that are visible to those who might want to violate our security, such as guards, dogs, well-lit areas, fences, and other similar measures, our would-be criminal might decide we are too difficult a target to be worth the effort.

Detective

Detective controls serve to detect and report undesirable events that are taking place. The classic example of a detective control can be found in burglar alarms and physical intrusion detection systems. Such systems typically monitor for indicators of unauthorized activity, such as doors or windows opening, glass being broken, movement, and temperature changes, and also can be in place to monitor for undesirable environmental conditions such as flooding, smoke and fire, electrical outages, excessive carbon dioxide in the air, and so on.

We may also see detective systems in the form of human or animal guards, whether they are physically patrolling an area or monitoring secondhand through the use of technology such as camera systems. This type of monitoring has both good and bad points, in that a living being may be technically less focused than an electronic system, but does have the potential to become distracted and will need to be relieved for meals, bathroom breaks, and other similar activities. Additionally, we can scale such guards from the lowliest unarmed security guard to highly trained and well-armed security forces, as is appropriate for the situation. As is true for most implementations involving security, the principle of defense in depth, as we discussed in Chapter 1, applies here.

Preventive

Preventive controls are used to physically prevent unauthorized entities from breaching our physical security. An excellent example of preventive security can be found in the simple mechanical lock. Locks are nearly ubiquitous for securing various facilities against unauthorized entry, including businesses, residences, and other locations.

In addition to locks, we can also see preventive controls in the form of high fences, bollards (the brightly painted and cement-filled posts that are placed to prevent vehicles from driving into buildings), and, once again, guards and dogs. We may also see preventive controls focused specifically on people, vehicles, or other particular areas of concern, depending on the environment in question.

How We Use Physical Access Controls

Preventive controls are generally the core of our security efforts, and in some cases, they may be the only effort and the only physical security control actually in place. We can commonly see this in residences, where there are locks on the doors, but no alarm systems or any other measures that might deter a criminal from gaining unauthorized entry.

In commercial facilities, we are much more likely to see all three types of controls implemented, in the form of locks, alarm systems, and signs indicating the presence of the alarm systems. Following the principles of defense in depth, the more layers we put in place for physical security, the better-off we will be.

Another important consideration in implementing physical security is to only put security in place that is reasonably consistent with the value of what we are protecting. If we have an empty warehouse, it does not make sense to put in high-security locks, alarm systems, and armed guards. Likewise, if we have a house full of expensive computers and electronics, it does not make sense to equip it with cheap locks and forgo an alarm system entirely.

PROTECTING PEOPLE

The primary concern of physical security is to protect the individuals on which our business depends and those that are close to us. While we put security measures and backup systems in place to ensure that our facilities, equipment, and data remain in functional condition, if we lose the people we depend on to work with the equipment and data, we have a rather difficult problem to solve. In many cases, we can restore our data from backups, we can build new facilities if they become destroyed or damaged, and we can buy new equipment; but replacing experienced people beyond the one or two at a time that we find with normal turnover is difficult, if not impossible, within any reasonable period of time.

Physical Concerns for People

As people are rather fragile in comparison to equipment, they can be susceptible to nearly the entire scope of threats we discussed at the beginning of this chapter. Extreme temperatures, or even not so extreme temperatures, can quickly render a person very uncomfortable, at best.

In the case of liquids, gases, or toxins, the absence, presence, or incorrect proportion of a variety of them can be harmful to individuals. We can very clearly see how a liquid such as water, in excessive quantities, might be an undesirable thing, as we saw in the case of the massive flooding that took place in the southern United States during Hurricane Katrina in 2005. Likewise, the lack of a gas such as oxygen, or too much of the same, can become deadly to people very quickly. Although we can see where harm might come from a toxin being introduced to an environment very clearly, a number of common substances may already be present, but are not toxic in the quantities or mixtures in which they are commonly used. We might see certain chemicals as being beneficial when they are used to filter the water in our facilities, but the same might not be true if the chemical ratios or mixtures are changed.

Any variety of living organisms can be dangerous to people, from larger animals, to insects, to nearly invisible molds, fungi, or other microscopic organisms. People can suffer from contact with living organisms in a variety of ways, from being bitten or stung by various critters, to developing breathing problems from inhaling mold.

Movement can be very harmful to people, particularly when said movement is the result of an earthquake, mudslide, avalanche, building structural issue, or other similar problems. In most cases, such threats can be both very harmful and very difficult to protect against.

Energy anomalies, are, of course, very dangerous to people. We might find equipment with poorly maintained shielding or insulation, or mechanical and/or electrical faults that could expose people to microwaves, electricity, radio waves, infrared light, radiation, or other harmful emissions. The results of such exposures may be immediately obvious, in the case of an electric shock, or they may be very long term, in the case of exposure to radiation.

People, of course, are one of the most severe threats against other people. There are an endlessly variable number of ways that other people can cause us trouble as we plan for the safety of our own. We might encounter civil unrest as a real possibility in certain parts of the world. We could encounter social engineering attacks, in an effort to extract information from our personnel or to gain unauthorized access to facilities or data through them. Our people could be physically attacked in a dark parking lot, or subjected to other similar circumstances. We can also add projectiles into this category, as people-harming projectiles are often launched at the behest of other people.

Smoke and fire can also be very dangerous to people in the sense of burns, smoke inhalation, temperature issues, and other similar problems. Particularly in the case of large facilities, smoke and fire can render the physical layout of the area very confusing or impassible, and can make it very difficult for our personnel to navigate their way to safety. We may also see the issue compounded by supplies, infrastructure, or the fabric of the building itself reacting in an unfavorable way and releasing toxins, collapsing, or producing the threats we have discussed in this section.

Safety

As we mentioned at the beginning of the chapter, the safety of people is the first and foremost concern on our list when we plan for physical security.

Safety of people falls above any other concern and must be prioritized above saving equipment or data, even when such actions will directly cause such items to be damaged.

We might find an example of this in the fire suppression systems in use in some data centers. In many cases, the chemicals, gases, or liquids that are used to extinguish fires in such environments are very harmful to people and may kill them if used in such an environment. For this reason, fire suppression systems are often equipped with a safety override that can prevent them from being deployed if there are people in the area. If we were to prevent the suppression system from extinguishing the fire because we knew a person was still in the data center, we might lose all the equipment in the data center, and potentially data that we could not replace. This would still be the correct choice to make with human life at stake.

Likewise, if we are in a facility where an emergency is taking place, our priority should be the evacuation of the facility, not the safety of the equipment.

Evacuation

Evacuation is one of the best methods we can use to keep our people safe. In almost any dangerous situation, an orderly evacuation away from the source of danger is the best thing we can do. There are a few main principles to consider when planning an evacuation: where, how, and who.

WHERE

Where we will be evacuating to is an important piece of information to consider in advance, whether we are evacuating a commercial building or a residence. We need to get everyone to the same place to ensure that they are at a safe distance and that we can account for everyone. If we do not do this in an orderly and consistent fashion, we may end up with a variety of issues. In commercial buildings, evacuation meeting places are often marked with signs, and on evacuation maps.

HOW

Also of importance is the route we will follow to reach the evacuation meeting place. When planning such routes, we should consider where the nearest exit from a given area can be reached, as well as alternate routes if some routes are impassable in an emergency. We should also avoid the use of areas that are dangerous or unusable in emergencies, such as elevators or areas that might be blocked by automatically closing fire doors.

WHO

The most vital portion of the evacuation, of course, is to ensure that we actually get everyone out of the building, and that we can account for everyone at the evacuation meeting place. This process typically requires at least two people to be responsible for any given group of people: one person to ensure that everyone he or she is responsible for has actually left the building and another at the meeting place to ensure that everyone has arrived safely.

PRACTICE

Particularly in large facilities, a full evacuation can be a complicated prospect. In a true emergency, if we do not evacuate quickly and properly, a great number of lives may be lost. As an unfortunate attestation to this, we can look to the example of the 2001 attacks on the World Trade Center in the United States, as shown in Figure 7.3.

A study conducted in 2008 determined that only 8.6 percent of the people in the buildings actually evacuated when the alarms were sounded. The rest remained in the buildings, gathering belongings, shutting down computers, and performing other such tasks [2]. It is important that we train our personnel to evacuate safely, and to respond quickly and properly when the signal to evacuate has been given.

Administrative Controls

We may, and likely will, also have a variety of administrative controls in place to protect people, in addition to the physical measures we put in place. Administrative controls are usually based on rules of some variety. More specifically, they may be policies, procedures, guidelines, regulations, laws, or similar bodies, and may be instituted at any level from informal company policies to federal laws.

FIGURE 7.3
North Tower of the World Trade Center, September 11, 2001 [1]

Companies put several common practices in place specifically to protect our people and our interests in general. One of the most common is the background check. When an individual has made it far enough through the hiring process that it seems likely he or she will be hired, the hiring company will often institute a background check. A number of companies globally carry out such background checks, including AccuScreen and LexisNexis. Such investigations will typically involve checks for criminal history, verification of previous employment, verification of education, credit checks, drug testing, and other items, depending on the position being pursued.

We may also conduct a variety of reoccurring checks on those in our employ. One of the more common and well-known examples can be seen in the drug tests conducted by certain employers. We may also see any of the checks we discussed as being common at the initiation of employment repeated in a similar fashion. Whether such checks occur or not often depends on the specific employer in question, and some employers may not conduct them at all.

The other areas in which we may see similar types of checks are when a person is terminated from employment, or perhaps when he or she leaves voluntarily. Here, we may see an exit interview take place, a process to ensure that the employee has returned all company property and that any accesses to systems or areas have been revoked. We may also ask the individual to sign paperwork agreeing not to pursue legal action against the company, additional nondisclosure agreements (NDAs), and other agreements, varying by the position as well as local or federal laws.

PROTECTING DATA

Second only to the safety of our personnel is the safety of our data. As we discussed in Chapter 5, one of our primary means of protecting data is the use of encryption. Although this is a reasonably sure solution, certain attacks may render it useless, such as those that break the encryption algorithm itself, or use other means to obtain the encryption keys. Following the concept of defense in depth that we covered in Chapter 1, another layer of security we need to ensure is the physical element. If we keep our physical storage media physically safe against attackers, unfavorable environmental conditions, or other threats that might harm them, we place ourselves on a considerably more sound security footing.

Physical Concerns for Data

Depending on the type of physical media on which our data is stored, any number of adverse physical conditions may be problematic or harmful to their integrity. Such media are often sensitive to temperature, humidity, magnetic fields, electricity, impact, and more, with each type of media having its particular strong and weak points.

Magnetic media, whether we refer to hard drives, tapes, floppy disks, or otherwise, generally involves some variety of movement and magnetically sensitive material on which the data is recorded. The combination of magnetic sensitivity and moving parts often makes such storage media fragile in one way or another. In most cases, strong magnetic fields can harm the integrity of data stored on magnetic media, with media outside of metal casing, such as magnetic tapes, being even more sensitive to such disruption. Additionally, jolting such media while it is in motion, typically while it is being read from or written to, can have a variety of undesirable effects, often rendering the media unusable.

Flash media, referring to the general category of media that stores data on non-volatile memory chips, is actually rather hardy in nature. If we can avoid impacts that might directly crush the chips on which the data is stored and we do not expose them to electrical shocks, they will generally withstand conditions that many other types of media will not. They are not terribly sensitive to temperature ranges below what would actually destroy the housing, and will often survive brief immersion in liquid, if properly dried afterward. Some flash drives are designed specifically to survive extreme conditions that would normally destroy such media, for those that might consider such conditions to be a potential issue.

Optical media, such as CDs and DVDs, is fairly fragile, as those with small children can attest to. Even small scratches on the surface of the media may render it unusable. It is also very temperature sensitive, being constructed largely of plastic and thin metal foil. Outside of a protected environment, such as a purpose-built media storage vault, any of a variety of threats may destroy the data on such media.

An additional factor that can potentially cause concern when dealing with storage media over an extended period of time is that of technical obsolescence. Type of storage media, software, interfaces, and other factors can affect our ability to read stored data. For example, at the time of this writing, Sony is planning to end production of floppy diskettes in March 2011, after having been responsible for 70 percent of the remaining production of such media [3]. Although floppy diskettes are only now completely fading from use, many new computers no longer come equipped with drives to read them. In a few short years, finding hardware to read these disks will become very difficult indeed.

Availability

One of our larger concerns when we discuss protecting data is to ensure that the data is available to us when we need to access it. The availability of our data often hinges on both our equipment and our facilities remaining in functioning condition, as we discussed earlier, and the media on which our data is stored being in working condition. Any of the physical concerns we discussed earlier can render our data inaccessible, in the sense of being able to read it from the media on which it is stored.

Although we are specifically discussing access to data here, and we talked about some of the potential hardware issues in accessing certain types of media earlier, there is also a fairly substantial equipment and infrastructure component to consider when discussing availability. Not only can we experience issues in reading the data from the media, but we may also have problems in getting to where the data is stored. If we are experiencing an outage, whether it is related to network, power, computer systems, or other components, at any point between our location and a remote data location, we may not be able to access our data remotely. Many businesses operate globally today, and it is possible that the loss of ability to access data remotely, even temporarily, will be a rather serious issue.

Residual Data

When we look at the idea of keeping data safe, we not only need to have the data available when we need access to it, but we also must be able to render the data inaccessible when it is no longer required. In some cases, this need is relatively obvious; for instance, we might not overlook the need to shred a stack of paper containing sensitive data before we throw it away. But the data stored on electronic media may not present itself so clearly to everyone that might be handling it or disposing of it.

In many cases, we can find stored data in several computing-related devices, such as computers, disk arrays, portable media devices, flash drives, backup tapes, CD or DVD media, and similar items. We would hope that the relatively computer savvy people would realize the media or device might contain some sensitive data, and that they should erase the data before they dispose of it. Unfortunately, this is not always the case.

In the early 2000s, a study was conducted on more than 150 used hard drives purchased from a variety of different sources, with a large number of them being purchased from eBay. When the contents of the disks were analyzed, it was discovered that many of them still contained data, to include medical data, pornography, e-mail messages, and several disks that appeared to have been used for financial data containing more than 6,500 credit card numbers [4]. In many cases, no attempt had been made to erase the data from the disks.

In addition to the devices that obviously contain storage and may hold potentially sensitive data, there are a variety of other places that we might find stored data. Although they may not immediately appear to be computing devices, a broad variety of office equipment such as copiers, printers, and fax machines may contain volatile or nonvolatile internal storage, often in the form of a hard drive. On such storage media, we can often find copies of the documents that have been processed by the drive, to include sensitive business data. When these types of devices are retired from service, or are sent for repair, we may not always think to remove the data from the storage media, and as such, we may be exposing data that we would not normally want made public.

Backups

In order to ensure that we can maintain the availability of our data, we will likely want to maintain backups. Not only do we need to back up the data itself, but we also need to maintain backups of the equipment and infrastructure that are used to provide access to the data.

We can perform data backups in a number of ways. We can utilize redundant arrays of inexpensive disks (RAID) in a variety of configurations to ensure that we do not lose data from hardware failures in individual disks, we can replicate data from one machine to another over a network, or we can make copies of data onto backup storage media, such as DVDs or magnetic tapes.

MORE ADVANCED

RAID, often redundantly referred to as RAID arrays, was developed in the late 1980s at the University of California at Berkeley [5]. There are a number of different ways to configure RAID, but the ultimate goal is to copy data to more than one storage device in order to prevent the loss of any one device from destroying its stored data. The original RAID paper describing the basic concepts, "A case for redundant arrays of inexpensive disks (RAID)," can be read at the Association for Computing Machinery (ACM) Digital Library.

PROTECTING EQUIPMENT

Last on the list of our concerns for physical security, although still very important and significant, is protecting our equipment, and, to a certain extent, the facilities that house it. This category falls last on the list because it represents the easiest and cheapest segment of our assets to replace. Even in the case of a major disaster that completely destroys our facility and all the computing equipment inside it, as long as we still have the people needed to run our operation and are able to restore or access our critical data, we can be back in working order very shortly. Replacing floor space or relocating to another area nearby can generally be accomplished with relative ease, and computing equipment is both cheap and plentiful. Although it may take us some time to be back to the same state we were in before the incident, getting to a bare minimum working state technology-wise is often a simple, if arduous, task.

Physical Concerns for Equipment

The physical threats that might harm our equipment, although fewer than those we might find harmful to people, are still numerous.

Extreme temperatures can be very harmful to equipment. We typically think of heat as being the most harmful to computing equipment, and this is largely correct. In environments that contain large numbers of computers and associated equipment, such as in a data center, we rely on environmental conditioning equipment to keep the temperature down to a reasonable level, typically in the high-60s to mid-70s on the Fahrenheit scale, although there is some debate over the subject [6].

Liquids can be very harmful to equipment, even when in quantities as small as those that can be found in humid air. Depending on the liquid in question, and the quantity of it present, we may find corrosion in a variety of devices, short circuits in electrical equipment, and other harmful effects. Clearly, in extreme cases, such as we might find in flooding, such equipment will often be rendered completely unusable after having been immersed.

Living organisms can also be harmful to equipment, although in the environments with which we will typically be concerned, these will often be of the smaller persuasion. Insects and small animals that have gained access to our equipment may cause electrical shorts, interfere with cooling fans, chew on wiring, and generally wreak havoc.

> **NOTE**
>
> The term *bug* being used to indicate a problem in a computer system originated in September 1947. In this case, a system being tested was found to have a moth shorting two connections together and causing the system to malfunction. When the moth was removed, the system was described as having been debugged [7], and the actual "bug" in question can be seen in Figure 7.4. 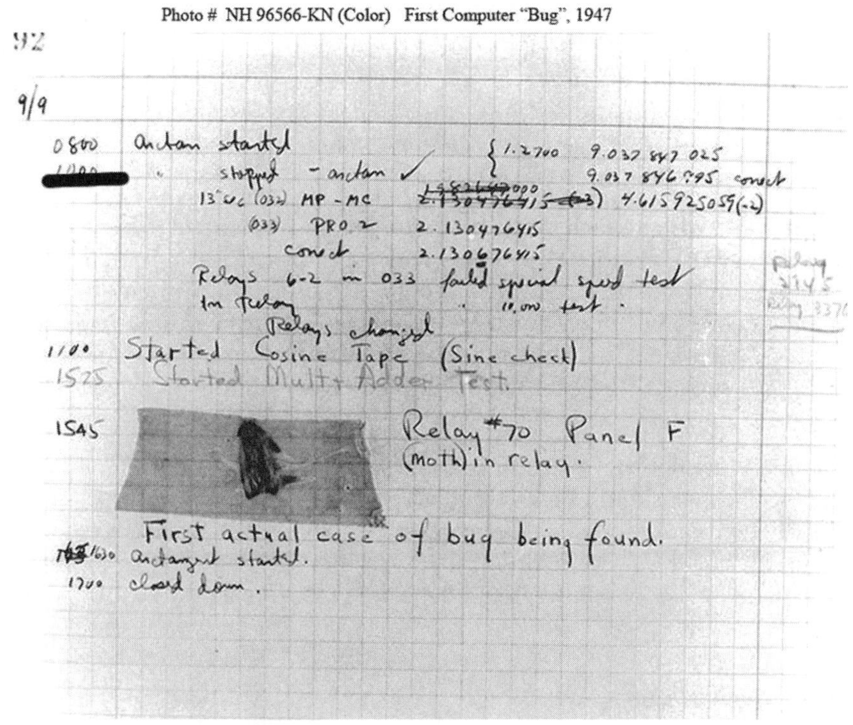
>
>
> **FIGURE 7.4**
> The First Bug [8]

Movement in earth and in the structure of our facilities can be a very bad thing for our equipment. One of the more obvious examples we can look at is an earthquake. Not only can earthquakes cause structural damage to our facilities, but the resultant shaking, vibrations, and potential for impacts due to structural failures can cause a large amount of damage.

Energy anomalies can be extremely harmful to any type of electrical equipment in a variety of ways. If we see issues with power being absent or temporarily not sending the expected amount of voltage, our equipment may be damaged beyond repair as a result. Good facility design will provide some measure of protection against such threats, but we generally cannot completely mitigate the effects of severe electrical issues, such as lightning strikes.

Smoke and fire are very bad for our equipment, as they introduce a number of harmful conditions. With smoke or fire, we might experience extreme temperatures, electrical issues, movement, liquids, and a variety of other problems. Efforts to extinguish fires, depending on the methods used, may also cause as much harm as the fire itself.

Site Selection

When we are planning a new facility, or selecting a new location to which to move, we should be aware of the area in which the facility will be located. A number of factors could cause us issues in terms of protecting our equipment and may impact the safety of our people and data as well. If the site is located in an area prone to natural disasters such as floods, storms, tornadoes, mudslides, or similar issues, we may find our facility to be completely unusable or destroyed at some point.

Similar issues might include areas that have the potential for civil unrest, unstable power or utilities, poor network connectivity, extreme temperature conditions, and so forth. With the proper facility design, we may be able to compensate for some problems without great difficulty, by installing power filtering and generators in order to compensate for power problems, for instance, but others, such as the local temperature, we may ultimately not be able to mitigate to any great extent.

Although potential site selection issues may not completely preclude our use of the facility, we should be aware that they may cause us problems and plan for such occurrences. For certain types of facilities, such as data centers, for instance, it may be very important for us to have as problem-free of an environment as we can possibly select, and, in the case of such site issues, we may want to look elsewhere.

Securing Access

When we discuss securing access to our equipment or our facility, we return again to the concept of defense in depth. There are multiple areas, inside and outside, where we may want to place a variety of security measures, depending on the environment. A military installation may have the highest level of security available, whereas a small retail store may have the lowest level.

We can often see measures for securing physical access implemented on the perimeter of the property on which various facilities sit. Very often, we will at least see minimal measures in place to ensure that vehicle traffic is controlled and does not enter undesirable places. Such measures may take the form of security landscaping. For example, we may see trees, large boulders, large cement planters, and the like placed in front of buildings or next to driveways in order to prevent vehicle entry. At more secure facilities, we might see fences, concrete barriers, and other more obvious measures. Such controls are generally in place as deterrents, and may be preventive in nature as well.

At the facility itself, we will likely see some variety of locks, whether mechanical or electronic with access badges, in place on the doors entering the building. A typical arrangement for nonpublic buildings is for the main entrance of the building to be unlocked during business hours and a security guard or receptionist stationed inside. In more secure facilities, we are likely to see all doors locked at all times, and a badge or key required to enter the building. Typically, once inside the building, visitors will have limited access to a lobby area, and, perhaps, meeting and restrooms, whereas those authorized to enter the rest of the building will use a key or badge to access it.

Once inside the facility, we will often see a variety of physical access controls, depending on the work and processes being carried out. We may see access controls on internal doors or individual floors of the building in order to keep visitors or unauthorized people from freely accessing the entire facility. Very often, in the case where computer rooms or data centers are present, access to them will be restricted to those that specifically need to enter them for business reasons. We may also find more complex physical access controls in place in such areas, such as biometric systems.

Environmental Conditions

For the equipment within our facilities, maintaining proper environmental conditions can be crucial to continued operations. Computing equipment can be very sensitive to changes in power, temperature, and humidity, as well as electromagnetic disturbances. Particularly in areas where we have large quantities of equipment, such as we might find in a data center, maintaining the proper conditions can be challenging, to say the least.

When facilities that will contain equipment sensitive to such conditions are constructed, they are often equipped with the means to provide emergency electrical power, often in the form of generators, as well as systems that can heat, cool, and moderate the humidity, as required. Outside of locations that are so equipped, our equipment will be at considerably greater risk of malfunction and damage. Unfortunately, such controls can be prohibitively expensive and we may not find smaller facilities appropriately equipped.

PHYSICAL SECURITY IN THE REAL WORLD

Physical security is a fact of daily life in both our business and personal lives. The physical controls we discussed can be seen in use in many environments. We can see locks, fences, cameras, security guards, lighting, and other such measures all over the world, in nearly any area we care to look. In higher security environments, we can begin to see more complex security measures, such as the use of iris scanners, mantraps (think a phone booth with two doors that lock), identification badges equipped to store certificates, and other such tools.

We can also see examples of measures that are put in place to protect people in almost any office building or public building we walk into. We can almost always find evacuation routes posted in the form of maps throughout the facility to indicate the different routes, as well as signage indicating meeting places in the case of an evacuation. We can also see administrative controls in place specifically to protect people in the background checks that most companies run when hiring, and the periodic tests that are run in some environments to test for drug use. One of the best examples of this type of administrative control can be found in the militaries of various countries. Such institutions often conduct background checks that are far more rigorous than we would ever find outside of such an environment, and they continue to do so on an ongoing basis through the careers of their members.

Protecting data is a large concern in any business or institution based on the use of technology. The idea of keeping backups for data is an institution in the world of information technology and is a given for most organizations. Unfortunately, this is not also the case for securing the media on which data is stored. Although this is not a universal issue, it is frequent enough that we see security breaches often in the media related to missing backup tapes, stolen laptops, and the like. The concept of residual data has also risen quite a bit higher in public view lately, with people becoming more aware of the possibility of data remaining behind on a variety of storage devices, even after attempts have been made to erase or format the media.

Protecting equipment and facilities is another concept with fairly ubiquitous acceptance in most commercial industries. The idea that we need to secure buildings, set guards where appropriate, and apply any other security measures that are appropriate to the value of what we are protecting is implicit. This is understandable, as the concept of physical security for protecting facilities and equipment is a truly ancient one. We can also see the idea of site selection for security reasons quite far back in history. The idea of maintaining environmental conditions in order to facilitate computing environments is rather new, however, and is also very common in business. Many office buildings are equipped with the large environmental and power conditioning systems that are required for such efforts, particularly those that were built with the inclusion of a data center in mind.

SUMMARY

Physical security controls, to include deterrent, detective, and preventive measures, are the means we put in place to mitigate physical security issues. Deterrents aim to discourage those that might violate our security, detective measures alert us to or allow us to detect when we have a potential intrusion, and preventive controls actually prevent intrusions from taking place. In isolation, none of these controls is a complete solution, but together, they can put us on a much stronger footing for physical security.

Protecting people is the foremost concern when planning our physical security. Although data and equipment can generally be replaced, when proper precautions are taken, people can be very difficult to replace. People are fragile creatures, and one of the best steps we can take when faced with a situation where they might be harmed is to remove them from the dangerous situation. Additionally, we may implement a variety of administrative controls in order to keep them safe in their working environments.

Protecting data, second only to protecting our people, is a highly critical activity in our world of technology-based business. One of our primary concerns with data is being able to ensure its availability when it is needed, and another is being able to ensure that we can completely delete it when we no longer desire to keep it. One of our main methods of ensuring availability is to perform backups, whether this is through the use of RAID to protect against storage media failures, or backups onto removable media such as DVDs or magnetic tape.

Protecting our equipment, although the lowest of the three categories on our priority list, is still a vital task. When we select the site for our facility, we need to take into account the threats that might be relevant to the location, and take steps to mitigate them. We also need to take the necessary steps to secure access outside, to, and within our facility. We have to protect our equipment not only from those that would intrude from the outside but also from those that have legitimate access to the facility, but not to certain areas within it. Lastly, we need to maintain the appropriate environmental conditions for our equipment to function, largely power, temperature, and humidity.

EXERCISES

1. Name the three major concerns for physical security, in order of importance.
2. Name the three main categories in which we are typically concerned with physical security.
3. Why might we want to use RAID?
4. What is the foremost concern as related to physical security?
5. What type of physical access control might we put in place in order to block access to a vehicle?
6. Give three examples of a physical control that constitutes a deterrent.
7. Give an example of how a living organism might constitute a threat to our equipment.
8. Which category of physical control might include a lock?
9. What is residual data and why is it a concern when protecting the security of our data?
10. What is our primary tool for protecting people?

Bibliography

[1] U.S. Environmental Protection Agency, Trade center photograph, New York. <http://www.epa.gov/wtc/pictureshtml>, 2001.

[2] N.C. McConnell, K.E. Boyce, J. Shields, E.R. Galea, R.C. Day, and L.M. Hulse. The UK 9/11 evacuation study: analysis of survivors' recognition and response phase in WTC1, Fire Saf. J. 45 (1) (2008) 21–34.

[3] S. Musil, Sony delivers floppy disk's last rites, Cnet News, <http://news.cnet.com/8301-1001_3-20003360-92.html>, April 25, 2010 (accessed: January 27, 2011).

[4] S.L. Garflinkel, S. Abhi, Remembrance of data passed: a study of disk sanitization practices, IEEE Secur. Priv. 3 (1) (2003) 1540–7993.

[5] D.A. Patterson, G. Garth, and H.K. Randy, A case for redundant arrays of inexpensive disks (RAID), Association for Computing Machinery. <http://portal.acm.org/citation.cfm?id=50214>, 1988.

[6] R. Miller, Data center cooling set points debated, Data Center Knowledge, <http://www.datacenterknowledge.com/archives/2007/09/24/data-center-cooling-set-points-debated/>, September 24, 2007 (accessed: January 27, 2011).

[7] Rear Admiral Grace Murray Hopper, USNR (1906–1992), Naval history and heritage command. <http://www.history.navy.mil/photos/pers-us/uspers-h/g-hoppr.htm>, 2011 (accessed: January 27, 2010).

[8] Naval Surface Warfare Center, Photo #NH 96566-KN (Color), Naval Surface Warfare Center Computer Museum, Dahlgren, VA, 1988.

CHAPTER 8

Network Security

Information in This Chapter:

- Protecting Networks
- Protecting Network Traffic
- Network Security Tools

INTRODUCTION

In the world of network security, we may face a number of threats from attackers, from misconfigurations of infrastructure or network-enabled devices, or even from simple outages. As network dependent as the majority of the world is, loss of network connectivity, and loss of the services that such networks provide, can be suffocating, at best, and can be potentially devastating to businesses.

In early 2011, civil unrest in Egypt reached a high point, with a large portion of the Egyptian population clamoring for a regime change away from long-time President Hosni Mubarak. In what was presumably an effort to somewhat quell public rebellion and communication both within Egypt and to the outside world regarding the situation, the Egyptian government deliberately disconnected almost the entire country from the global networks that comprise the Internet. The majority of cellular communications networks were also taken down in conjunction with this [1]. Egypt remained off-line for several days, before access was restored. It is difficult to quantify the effects of such a large-scale outage in the modern world, particularly since this is the first such intentional outage of this scale.

Although the situation in Egypt may be an extreme example, we can see serious impact from the wide variety of smaller network outages and issues that occur all over the world every day. Some of these problems may be the result of technical issues, some may be the result of distributed denial of service (DDoS) attacks (discussed later in this chapter), and some may be temporary and due to causes entirely unknown to the network users.

In this chapter, we will discuss some of the issues in protecting networks, and the various infrastructure and devices we might put in place to do so. We will also talk about protecting network traffic as it moves over networks, and some of the tools we might use to verify our security.

PROTECTING NETWORKS

We can look to a variety of avenues to protect our networks and network resources against the array of threats we might face. We can add security in the form of network design by laying out our networks in a fashion that makes them inherently more secure and resistant to attack or technical mishap. We can also implement a variety of devices at the borders of and within our networks to increase our level of security, such as firewalls and intrusion detection systems (IDSes).

Security in Network Design

Proper network design provides us with one of the chief tools we have to protect ourselves from the variety of network threats we might face. With a properly laid out network, we can prevent some attacks entirely, mitigate others, and, when we can do nothing else, fail in a graceful way.

Network segmentation can go a long way toward reducing the impact of such attacks. When we segment a network, we divide it into multiple smaller networks, each acting as its own small network called a subnet. We can control the flow of traffic between subnets, allowing or disallowing traffic based on a variety of factors, or even blocking the flow of traffic entirely if necessary. Properly segmented networks can boost network performance by containing certain traffic to the portions of the network that actually need to see it, and can help to localize technical network issues. Additionally, network segmentation can prevent unauthorized network traffic or attacks from reaching portions of the network to which we would prefer to prevent access, as well as making the job of monitoring network traffic considerably easier.

Another design factor that can be of assistance in the name of securing our networks is to funnel network traffic through certain points where we can inspect, filter, and control the traffic, often referred to as choke points. The choke points might be the routers that move traffic from one subnet to another, the firewalls or proxies that control traffic moving within, into, or out of our networks or portions of our networks, or the application proxies that filter the traffic for particular applications such as Web or e-mail traffic. We will discuss some of these devices at greater length in the next section of this chapter.

Redundancy in network design can prove to be another major factor in helping to mitigate issues on our networks. Certain technical issues or attacks may render unusable portions of our networks, network infrastructure devices, border devices such as firewalls, or a number of other components that contribute to the functionality of our networks. Good network design includes planned redundancy for devices failing, connectivity being lost, or coming under attack to the point that they are rendered useless or we lose control of them. For example, if one of our border devices is being subjected to a DDoS attack, there are few steps we can take to mitigate the attack. We can, however, switch to a different connection to the Internet, or route traffic through a different device until we can come to a longer-term solution.

Firewalls

A firewall is a mechanism for maintaining control over the traffic that flows into and out of our network(s). The concept and first implementations of firewall technologies can be traced back to the late 1980s and early 1990s. One of the first papers to discuss the idea of using a firewall is titled "Simple and Flexible Datagram Access Controls," written in 1989 by Jeffrey Mogul [2], then at Digital Equipment Corporation (DEC). We can also see the first commercial firewall from DEC, the DEC SEAL, which shipped in 1992 [3].

A firewall is typically placed in a network where we see the level of trust change. We might see a firewall on the border between our internal network and the Internet, as shown in Figure 8.1. We may also see a firewall put in place on our internal network to prevent network traffic of a sensitive nature from being accessed by those that have no reason to do so.

Many of the firewalls in use today are based on the concept of examining the packets that are coming in over the network. This examination determines what should be allowed in or out. Whether the traffic is allowed or blocked can be based on a variety of factors and largely depends on the complexity of the firewall. For example, we might allow or disallow traffic based on the protocol being used, allowing Web and e-mail traffic to pass, but blocking everything else.

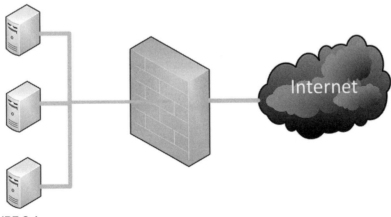

FIGURE 8.1
Firewall

PACKET FILTERING

Packet filtering is one of the oldest and simplest of firewall technologies. Packet filtering looks at the contents of each packet in the traffic individually and makes a gross determination, based on the source and destination IP addresses, the port number, and the protocol being used, of whether the traffic will be allowed to pass. Since each packet is examined individually and not in concert with the rest of the packets comprising the content of the traffic, it can be possible to slip attacks through this type of firewall.

STATEFUL PACKET INSPECTION

Stateful packet inspection firewalls (generally referred to as stateful firewalls) function on the same general principle as packet filtering firewalls, but they are able to keep track of the traffic at a granular level. While a packet filtering firewall only examines an individual packet out of context, a stateful firewall is able to watch the traffic over a given connection, generally defined by the source and destination IP addresses, the ports being used, and the already existing network traffic. A stateful firewall uses what is called a state table to keep track of the connection state and will only allow traffic through that is part of a new or already established connection. Most stateful firewalls can also function as a packet filtering firewall, often combining the two forms of filtering. For example, this type of firewall can identify and track the traffic related to a particular user-initiated connection to a Web site, and knows when the connection has been closed and further traffic should not legitimately be present.

DEEP PACKET INSPECTION

Deep packet inspection firewalls add yet another layer of intelligence to our firewall capabilities. Deep packet inspection firewalls are capable of analyzing the actual content of the traffic that is flowing through them. Although packet filtering firewalls and stateful firewalls can only look at the structure of the network traffic itself in order to filter out attacks and undesirable content, deep packet inspection firewalls can actually reassemble the contents of the traffic to look at what will be delivered to the application for which it is ultimately destined.

To use an analogy, if we ship a package via one of the common parcel carriers, the carrier will look at the size and shape of the package, how much it weighs, how it is wrapped, and the sending and destination addresses. This is generally what packet filter firewalls and stateful firewalls can do. Now, if the parcel carrier were to do all of this as well as open the package and inspect its contents, then make a judgment as to whether the package could be shipped based on its contents, this would be much more in line with deep packet inspection.

Although this technology has great promise for blocking a large number of the attacks we might see, the question of privacy is also raised. In theory, someone in control of a deep packet inspection device could read every one of our e-mail messages, see every Web page exactly as we saw it, and easily listen in on our instant messaging conversations.

PROXY SERVERS

Proxy servers are ultimately a specialized variant of a firewall. These servers provide security and performance features, generally for a particular application, such as mail or Web browsing. Proxy servers can serve as a choke point (discussed earlier in the chapter) in order to allow us to filter traffic for attacks or undesirable content such as malware or traffic to Web sites hosting adult content. They also allow us to log the traffic that goes through them for later inspection, and they serve to provide a layer of security for the devices behind them, by serving as a single source for requests.

Proxy servers are nearly ubiquitous in the business world, largely due to the filtering capability they provide. Many companies rely on them to keep the large amounts of spam that flow over e-mail from reaching their users and lowering productivity. We also see them used to filter Web traffic in such environments in order to keep employees from visiting Web sites that might have objectionable material, and to filter out traffic that might indicate the presence of malware.

DMZs

A DMZ, or demilitarized zone, is generally a combination of a network design feature and a protective device such as a firewall. As we discussed earlier in "Security in Network Design" section, we can often increase the level of security on our networks by segmenting them properly. When we look at systems that need to be exposed to external networks such as the Internet in order to function, such as mail servers and Web servers, we need to ensure their security and the security of the devices on the network behind them. We can often do this by putting a layer of protection between the device, such as our mail server, and the Internet, and between the rest of our network and the device, as shown in Figure 8.2.

This allows only the traffic that needs to reach the mail server—for instance, Internet Message Access Protocol (IMAP) and Simple Message Transfer

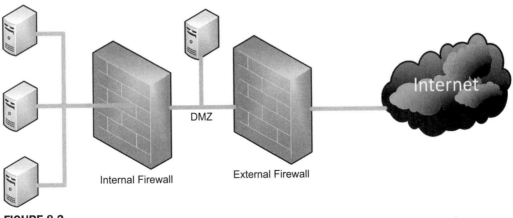

FIGURE 8.2
DMZ

Protocol (SMTP) on ports 143 and 25, respectively—to reach our mail server, and the same ports to pass through on our network. Presuming that no other services are running on the same system, we could restrict the traffic going into and out of the DMZ where our mail server sits to those particular ports.

Network Intrusion Detection

IDSes monitor the networks, hosts, or applications to which they are connected for unauthorized activity. There are several types of IDSes, including host-based intrusion detection systems (HIDSes), application protocol-based intrusion detection systems (APIDSes), and network-based intrusion detection systems (NIDSes). We will focus on NIDSes in this chapter, returning to HIDSes and APIDSes in Chapters 9 and 10, respectively.

NIDSes will typically be attached to the network in a location where they can monitor the traffic going by, but they need to be placed carefully so that they are not overloaded. Placing an NIDS behind another filtering device, such as a firewall, can help to eliminate some of the obviously spurious traffic in order to decrease the traffic the NIDS needs to inspect. As NIDSes need to examine a large amount of traffic on a typical network, they can generally do only a relatively cursory inspection in order to determine whether the situation on the network is normal or not. Because of this, an NIDS may miss some types of attacks, particularly those that are specifically crafted to pass through such inspections. Packet crafting attacks involve very specifically designed packets of traffic that carry attacks or malicious code, but are designed to avoid detection by IDSes, firewalls, and other similar devices.

IDS DETECTION METHODS

IDSes are often classified by the way they detect attacks. In general, they are divided into two main categories: signature-based detection and anomaly-based detection.

Signature-based IDSes work in a very similar fashion to most antivirus systems. They maintain a database of the signatures that might signal a particular type of attack and compare incoming traffic to those signatures. In general, this method works well, except when we encounter an attack that is new, or has been specifically constructed in order to not match existing attack signatures. One of the large drawbacks to this method is that many signature-based systems rely solely on their signature database in order to detect attacks. If we do not have a signature for the attack, we may not see it at all. In addition to this, the attacker crafting the traffic may have access to the same IDS tools we are using, and may be able to test the attack against them in order to specifically avoid our security measures.

The other major method of IDS detection is anomaly-based detection. Anomaly-based IDSes typically work by taking a baseline of the normal traffic and activity taking place on the network. They can measure the present state of traffic on the network against this baseline in order to detect patterns that are not present in the traffic normally. Such methods can work very well when we are looking to detect new attacks or attacks that have been deliberately assembled to avoid IDSes. On the other hand, we may also see larger numbers of false positives from anomaly-based IDSes than we might from signature-based IDSes. If the traffic on the network changes from what was present when we took our baseline, the IDS may see this as indicative of an attack, and likewise for legitimate activity that causes unusual traffic patterns or spikes in traffic.

We can, of course, put an IDS in place that gives us some of the advantages of each type of detection and use both the signature-based and anomaly-based methods in a single IDS. This will allow us much more flexibility in detecting attacks, although perhaps at the expense of operating a bit more slowly and causing a lag in detection.

PROTECTING NETWORK TRAFFIC

In addition to protecting our networks from intrusion, we also need to look to the traffic that flows over them. In line with the concept of defense in depth, we want to put in place as many layers of security as is reasonable for the value of what we are securing. Even when we are in an environment that we consider to be secure, we may be subject to a variety of attacks, and we would be foolish to not put protections in place in anticipation of such an eventuality occurring.

Intercepting Data

One of the largest concerns when we are sending sensitive data over a network is of having the data intercepted by someone that might misuse it. Given the many networks available today in offices, hotels, coffee shops, restaurants, and other places, the opportunity to accidentally expose data to an attacker is large.

When we send data over networks that are not secure or trusted, an eavesdropper can glean a large amount of information from what we send. If we use applications or protocols that do not encrypt what they are sending over the network, we may end up giving our login credentials, credit card numbers, banking information, and other data to anyone that happens to be listening.

Data can be intercepted from both wired and wireless networks, often with very little effort, depending on the design of the network. We will discuss some of the tools that can be used to perform such interception later in the chapter.

WIRELESS EXPOSURE

Wireless networks, in particular, are one of the major security risks when we consider places where our data might be exposed. Free wireless Internet access is commonly provided today in a number of places. Although it may be nice to be able to get network access for free, many people do not understand the security risk that accompanies such a service. In general, such networks are set up without a password and without encryption of any kind, which we would normally see in place in order to protect the confidentiality of the traffic flowing over the network. Even in cases where a password is required to access the network, such as we might find in a hotel, if everyone else in the hotel is on the network as well, they may be able to see our data.

Although such insecure networks are a security problem, they are not an insurmountable one. We will discuss one of the tools we might use to secure such connections in the next section.

Virtual Private Networks

The use of virtual private networks (VPNs) can provide us with a solution for sending sensitive traffic over unsecure networks. A VPN connection, often referred to as a tunnel, is an encrypted connection between two points. This is generally accomplished through the use of a VPN client application on one end of the connection, and a device called a VPN concentrator on the other end. The client uses the software to authenticate to the VPN concentrator, usually over the Internet, and after the connection has been established, all traffic exchanged from the network interface connected to the VPN flows through the encrypted VPN tunnel.

VPNs are often used to allow remote workers to connect to the internal resources of an organization. When such a connection has been established, the connected device is able to act as though it were connected directly to the internal network of the organization hosting the connection. This can be very useful as it allows us to enable greater access for a remote worker than we would normally be able to do securely when the worker is outside the borders of our network.

In addition to allowing us access to the internal resources of our organization, VPNs may also be used to protect or anonymize the traffic we are sending over untrusted connections. Companies such as StrongVPN sell their services to the public for exactly such purposes, allowing us to protect the contents of our traffic from logging by our Internet service providers (ISPs) or being sniffed by others on the same network, to obscure our geographical location and bypass location-oriented blocking.

Such services are also popular with those that engage in peer-to-peer (P2P) file-sharing services. Such activity is often flagged by ISPs and by organizations such as the Motion Picture Association of America (MPAA) and the Recording Industry Association of America (RIAA) in order to prosecute those engaged in copyright infringement. VPNs can allow both the traffic and the actual IP addresses of those that engage in such activities to remain hidden from those that would seek them out.

Wireless Network Security

As we discussed earlier in this chapter, unsecured wireless networks freely broadcast our data for anyone with the appropriate (and very common) technology to hear. The present record for an unamplified 802.11 wireless connection is about 237 miles [4]. Although this was under ideal conditions, it does give us some idea of how far our wireless signals might carry. This means that, even in a much less favorable radio frequency (RF) environment, such as we might find in a residential area, someone miles away could potentially be eavesdropping on our network traffic.

In addition to the issues with our traffic being potentially listened in on, there is also the possible issue of wireless devices being placed without our knowledge. In particular, wireless access points being attached to our network without authorization, commonly known as rogue access points, can present a serious security issue.

For example, if we worked in an area where wireless was prohibited, we might find that an enterprising individual decided to bring in an access point of his or her own and install it under his or her desk, in order to provide wireless access to a nearby outdoor smoking area. Although this might not have been done with bad intentions in mind, this one simple action may have invalidated the entire set of carefully planned network security measures we have put in place.

If the rogue access point in our example was set up with poor security or no security at all, our well-intentioned access point installer would have just provided anyone within range of the access point with an easy path directly into our network, bypassing any border security that we might have in place. There is a possibility that a network IDS might pick up the activity from the rogue access point, but there is no guarantee of this. The simple solution to finding such rogue equipment is to carefully document the legitimate devices that are part of the wireless network infrastructure, and regularly scan for additional devices using a tool such as Kismet, which we will discuss later in this chapter.

For the legitimate and authorized devices on our network, our chief method of protecting the traffic that flows through them is the use of encryption. The encryption used by 802.11 wireless devices, the most common of the wireless family of network devices, breaks down into three major categories: Wired Equivalent Privacy (WEP), Wi-Fi Protected Access (WPA), and Wi-Fi Protected Access version 2 (WPA2). Of these, WPA2 is the most current and offers the strongest inherent security.

Secure Protocols

One of the simplest and easiest ways we can protect our data is to use secure protocols. Many of the more common and older protocols, such as File Transfer Protocol (FTP) for transferring files, Telnet for interacting with remote machines, Post Office Protocol (POP) for retrieving e-mail, and a host of others, deal with data in an insecure manner. Such protocols often send sensitive information, such as logins and passwords, in cleartext (remember back to Chapter 5) over the network. Anyone listening on the network with a properly positioned sniffer can pick up the traffic from such protocols and easily glean the sensitive information from the traffic they send.

Many insecure protocols have secure equivalents, as we will discuss at greater length in Chapter 10. In brief, we can often find a secure protocol with the type of traffic we wish to carry. Instead of operating over the command line with Telnet, we can use Secure Shell (SSH), and instead of transferring files with FTP, we can use Secure File Transfer Protocol (SFTP), which is also based on SSH.

SSH is a very handy protocol for securing communications as we can send many types of traffic over it. It can be used for file transfers and terminal access, as we mentioned, and to secure traffic in a variety of other situations, such as when connecting to a remote desktop, communicating over a VPN, mounting remote file systems, and any number of other tasks. The encryption used by SSH is RSA, a public key encryption algorithm.

NETWORK SECURITY TOOLS

We can use a broad variety of tools to improve our network security. Many of these tools are the same as those used by attackers penetrating our networks, and this is one of the main reasons they are useful to us. We can use the same tools attackers use to penetrate our defenses in order to shore them up. By using such tools to locate security holes in our networks, we can patch up these holes to keep the attackers out.

MORE ADVANCED

An enormous number of security tools are on the market today, and many of them are free or have free alternatives. Many run on Linux operating systems, and some of them can be a bit difficult to configure. Fortunately, we can try out such tools without having to set them up by using one of the Security Live CD distributions that come with all of the tools preconfigured. One of the better-known and more thorough distributions is BackTrack, available for download at www.backtrack-linux.org/.

The key to using such an assessment strategy is to conduct assessments thoroughly and regularly enough that we are able to find the holes before the attackers do. If we only perform such testing, commonly known as penetration testing, on an occasional and shallow basis, we will likely not catch all the issues present in our environment. Additionally, as the various network hardware devices and the software running on them are updated, added, or removed over time, the vulnerabilities present in our environment will change as well. It is also important to note that the vast majority of the tools we might use will only be capable of finding known issues. New or unpublished attacks or vulnerabilities, commonly known as zero-day attacks, can still take us by surprise when they surface.

Wireless

As we discussed earlier in the chapter, attackers accessing a wireless device can potentially bypass all our carefully planned security measures. Worse yet, if we do not take steps to ensure that unauthorized wireless devices, such as rogue access points, are not put in place on our network, we could be allowing a large hole in our network security and never know it.

We can use several tools to detect wireless devices. One of the best known tools for detecting such devices is called Kismet, which runs on Linux and can be found on the BackTrack CD. Kismet is commonly used to detect wireless access points and can find them even when attempts have been made to make doing so difficult. A similar piece of software, called NetStumbler, exists for Windows, although it does not have as full a feature set as Kismet.

In addition to detecting wireless devices, some tools can enable us to break through the different varieties of encryption that are in use on such networks. Many tools for such purposes exist, but a few of the more common ones for cracking WEP, WPA, and WPA2 include coWPAtty and Aircrack-NG.

Scanners

Scanners are one of the mainstays of the security testing and assessment industry. We can generally break these into two main categories: port scanners and vulnerability scanners. There is some overlap between the two, depending on the particular tool we are talking about.

One of the more famous port scanners that we might want to use is a free tool called Nmap, short for network mapper. Although Nmap is generally referred to as a port scanner, we actually do it a bit of a disservice to call it that. Although Nmap can conduct port scans, it can also search for hosts on a network, identify the operating systems those hosts are running, detect the versions of the services running on any open ports, and much more.

For the most part, in terms of network security, scanners are the most useful when used as a tool for discovering the networks and systems that are in our environment. We will discuss some of the uses for scanners that are more specific to operating system security in Chapter 9.

Packet Sniffers

A network or protocol analyzer, also known as a packet sniffer, or just plain sniffer,[1] is a tool that can intercept traffic on a network, commonly referred to as sniffing. Sniffing basically amounts to listening for any traffic that the network interface of our computer or device can see, whether it was intended to be received by us or not.

---

[1] Sniffer is a registered trademark of Network General Corporation. We use the term *sniffer* in the generic sense in this book.

> ### ALERT!
> One of the key elements in employing a sniffer is to place it on the network in the proper position to allow us to actually see the traffic we would like to sniff. In most modern networks, the traffic is segmented in such a fashion that we will likely not be able to see much traffic at all, other than what we are generating from our own machine. In order to be able to sniff properly, we will likely need to gain access to one of the higher-level network switches, and may need to use specialized equipment or configurations to allow us access to our target traffic.

Tcpdump is a classic sniffing tool, and it has been around since the late 1980s. Tcpdump is a command-line tool that allows us to monitor the activities of the network to which we are attached, and has only a few other key features, such as filtering of traffic. Tcpdump runs only on UNIX-like operating systems, but a version has been ported to Windows, called WinDump.

Wireshark, previously known as Ethereal, is a fully featured sniffer that is capable of intercepting traffic from a wide variety of wired and wireless sources. It has a graphical interface, shown in Figure 8.3; it includes a large number

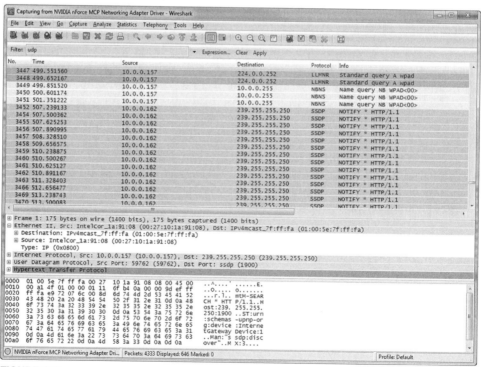

FIGURE 8.3
Wireshark

of filtering, sorting, and analysis tools; and it is one of the more popular sniffers on the market today.

Kismet, which we discussed in the "Wireless" section, is also a specialized sniffer. Although many of the other sniffers are network media agnostic, for the most part, Kismet will only sniff from wireless networks. Owing to this very specific focus, it can provide us with a much more specific set of tools.

We may also see packet sniffers in hardware form, such as the OptiView Portable Network Analyzer from Fluke Networks. Although we can definitely benefit from well-equipped portable analyzers such as this, they often tend to be very expensive and well beyond the budget of the average network or security professional.

Honeypots

Honeypots are a somewhat controversial tool in the arsenal of those we can use to improve our network security. A honeypot can detect, monitor, and sometimes tamper with the activities of an attacker. Honeypots are configured to deliberately display vulnerabilities or materials that would make the system attractive to an attacker. This might be an intentionally vulnerable service, an outdated and unpatched operating system, a network share named "top secret UFO documents," or other similar items that might serve as bait for an attacker.

One of the interesting things about honeypots is that the vulnerabilities or data that is left out to bait the attacker is entirely false. In reality, honeypots are configured to display these items so that we can catch the attackers, and monitor what they are doing on the system without their knowledge. This might be done in an effort to provide an early warning system for a corporation, as a method of researching what methods attackers are using, or as an intentional target to monitor the activities of malware in the wild.

We can also expand honeypots into larger structures by setting up several such systems in a network, often referred to as a honeynet. Honeynets can allow us to set up multiple honeypots with varying configurations and vulnerabilities, generally with some sort of centralized instrumentation for monitoring all the honeypots on the network. Honeynets can be particularly useful for large-scale monitoring of malware activity, as we can emulate a variety of different operating systems and vulnerabilities for our target systems to display.

ADDITIONAL RESOURCES

An excellent resource for more information on honeypots and honeynets is the Honeynet Project at www.honeynet.org/. The Honeynet Project provides access to a variety of resources, including software, the results of research, and numerous papers on the subject.

Firewall Tools

In our kit of network tools, we may also find it useful to include those that can map the topology of and help locate vulnerabilities in our firewalls. Hping3 is a well-known and useful tool for such efforts. It is able to construct specially crafted Internet Control Message Protocol (ICMP) packets in such a way as to evade some of the normal measures that are put in place to prevent us from seeing the devices that are behind a firewall. We can also script the activities of Hping3 in order to test the responses of firewalls and IDSes, so that we can get an idea of the rules on which they are operating.

We can also use a variety of the other tools we have discussed in this section to test the security of our firewalls. We can use port and vulnerability scanners to look at them from the outside in order to find any ports that are unexpectedly open, or any services running on our open ports that are vulnerable to known attacks. We can also use sniffers to examine the traffic that is entering and leaving firewalls, presuming that we can get such a tool in place in a network location that will enable us to see the traffic.

NETWORK SECURITY IN THE REAL WORLD

We can see the use of network security nearly everywhere in the world today. In businesses and in organizations, we can see concerted efforts at designing secure networks, including the implementation of firewalls and IDSes. Depending on the industry we are referring to, our business may depend entirely on the success of such measures in keeping us secure. If we look at network-focused companies such as eBay and Amazon, the vast majority of their business is conducted directly over the Internet. If they did not have rigid security measures in place, and they did not continuously evaluate them in order to find weaknesses, their businesses would quickly fail.

On the back end of such organizations, we can also find a variety of security measures that are put in place to keep the traffic and activities of their employees and users secure. Business use of VPN connections is very common, as this allows employees who are working from home or on the road to use internal network resources. We can also see the use of secure protocols when those that are outside the corporate firewalls are communicating with externally exposed servers in order to exchange e-mail, send files, communicate over instant messaging, and so forth.

As we mentioned, such companies also need to constantly evaluate their own security measures. We can use a number of tools to do so from a network perspective, including the few we discussed in this chapter, and many more. It is important to understand that such tools often do not fall cleanly across the lines of network security, operating system security, and application security, but often encompass one or more, if not all, of these aspects. This reflects the need to ensure security in all of these ways, and that these categories overlap heavily.

SUMMARY

When we protect our networks, we do so from a variety of different angles. We use secure network design to ensure that we have our networks segmented properly, that we have the proper choke points in order to allow monitoring and control of traffic, and that we are redundant where redundancy is needed. We also implement security devices such as firewalls and IDSes in order to protect us both inside and outside our networks.

In addition to protecting the networks themselves, we also need to look to protecting our network traffic. Owing to the nature of our networks, whether wired or wireless, it is often possible to eavesdrop on the traffic that travels over them. In order to protect our traffic, we can use VPNs to secure our connections when we use untrusted networks, we can use security measures specific to wireless networks when we need to use them, and we can make use of secure protocols as a general security measure.

In our efforts to provide for our network security, we may use a variety of security tools. When dealing with wireless networks, we can use tools that are specifically suited to such tasks, such as Kismet or NetStumbler. We can also listen in on network traffic with tools such as Wireshark or Tcpdump, scan for devices on our networks using tools such as Nmap, and test our firewalls using hping3 and other similar utilities. We can also place devices called honeypots on our networks specifically to attract the attention of attackers in order to study them and their tools and to alert us to their presence.

EXERCISES

1. For what might we use the tool Kismet?
2. Explain the concept of segmentation.
3. If we needed a command-line tool that could sniff network traffic, what tool might we use?
4. What are the three main types of wireless encryption?
5. What tool might we use to scan for devices on a network?
6. Why would we use a honeypot?
7. Explain the difference between signature and anomaly detection in IDSes.
8. What would we use if we needed to send sensitive data over an untrusted network?
9. What would we use a DMZ to protect?
10. What is the difference between a stateful firewall and a deep packet inspection firewall?

Bibliography

[1] J. Cowie, Egypt leaves the Internet. renesys.com. <http://www.renesys.com/blog/2011/01/egypt-leaves-the-internet.shtml>, January 27, 2011 (accessed: February 3, 2011).

[2] J. Mogul, Simple and flexible datagram access controls for Unix-based gateways, USENIX Conference Proceedings, 1989.

[3] K.J. Higgins, Who invented the firewall? Dark Reading. <www.darkreading.com/security/security-management/208803808/index.html>, January 15, 2008 (accessed: February 6, 2011).

[4] M. Kanellos, New Wi-Fi distance record: 382 kilometers, Cnet News. <http://news.cnet.com/8301-10784_3-9730708-7.html?part=rss&subj=news&tag=2547-1_3-0-5>, June 18, 2007 (accessed: February 6, 2011).

CHAPTER 9

Operating System Security

Information in This Chapter:

- Operating System Hardening
- Protecting against Malware
- Software Firewalls and Host Intrusion Detection
- Operating System Security Tools

INTRODUCTION

When we seek to protect our data, processes, and applications against concerted attacks, one of the largest areas in which we might find weaknesses is on the operating system that hosts all of these. If we do not take care to protect our operating systems, we really have no basis for getting to a reasonably strong security footing.

There are a number of ways by which we can mitigate the various threats and vulnerabilities we might face from an operating system perspective. One of the easiest categories we can point out is operating system hardening. We can use this technique when we are configuring hosts that might face hostile action in order to decrease the number of openings through which an attacker might ultimately reach us.

We can also add tools and applications to our operating system that are designed to combat some of the tools attackers might use against us. The most common and obvious of these is the use of anti-malware tools, which we will discuss later in this chapter, that protect us from the broad variety of malicious code to which our system might be exposed, particularly if it is Internet facing. In the same general class of software, we can also look to software firewalls and host-based intrusion detection systems (HIDSes) in order to block unwanted traffic and to alert us when undesirable network traffic is arriving at, or originating from, our systems.

We can also make use of the large number of security tools that are available to help us detect potentially vulnerable areas on our hosts. We might use such tools to find services that we did not know were running, locate network services that are known to contain exploitable flaws, and generally inspect our systems.

Through the combination of all these efforts, once again to return to the concept of defense in depth, we can mitigate many of the security issues we might find on the hosts for which we are responsible.

OPERATING SYSTEM HARDENING

When we look at operating system hardening, we arrive at a new concept in information security. One of the main goals of operating system hardening is to reduce the number of available avenues through which our operating system might be attacked. The total of these areas is referred to as our attack surface [1]. The larger our attack surface is, the greater chance we stand of an attacker successfully penetrating our defenses. Each area in which we are potentially insecure adds to our attack surface, and each area in which we have applied security measures decreases it.

There are six main ways in which we can decrease our attack surface, as listed here and shown in Figure 9.1:

- Removing unnecessary software
- Removing or turning off unessential services
- Making alterations to common accounts
- Applying the principle of least privilege
- Applying software updates in a timely manner
- Making use of logging and auditing functions

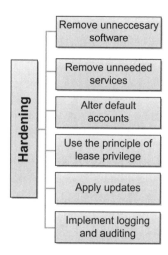

FIGURE 9.1
Six Main Hardening Categories

Remove All Unnecessary Software

> **ALERT!**
>
> We should always exercise great care when making changes to operating system settings, tools, and software. Some of the changes we might make could have unintended effects on the way our operating system functions, and a production machine is not the place to learn this through experience. Researching changes carefully before we make them is always a good idea.

Each piece of software installed on our operating system adds to our attack surface. Some software may have a much greater effect than others, but they all add up. If we are truly seeking to harden our operating system, we need to take a hard look at the software that should be loaded on it, and take steps to ensure that we are working with the bare minimum.

If we are preparing a Web server, for instance, we should have the Web server software, any libraries or code interpreters that are needed to support the Web server, and any utilities that deal with the administration and maintenance of the operating system, such as backup software, remote access tools, and so on. We really have no reason to install anything else if the system is truly going to function solely as a Web server.

Our problems begin to arise when we see other software installed on the machine, often with the best of intentions. For example, let us say that one of our developers logs in remotely and needs to make a change to a Web page on the fly, so they install the Web development software they need. Then they need to evaluate the changes, so they install their favorite Web browser and the associated media plug-ins, such as Adobe Flash and Acrobat Reader, as well as a video player to test the video content. In very short order, not only do we have software that should not be there, but the software quickly becomes outdated since it is not patched or updated, because it is not "officially" installed. At this point, we have a relatively serious security issue on an Internet-facing machine.

Remove All Unessential Services

In the same vein as removing unneeded software, we should also remove or disable unessential services. Many operating systems ship with a wide variety of services turned on in order to share information over the network, locate other devices, synchronize the time, allow files to be accessed and transferred, and perform other tasks. We may also find that services have been installed by various applications, to provide the tools and resources on which the application depends in order to function.

Turning operating services off can be an exercise in experimentation and frustration. In many cases, such services are not named in a fashion that indicates their actual function, and tracking down what each of them is doing may require a bit of research. One of the best things to do first when we are seeking to locate such extraneous services is to determine the network ports on which the system is actually listening for network connections. Many operating systems have built-in utilities that will allow us to do this, such as netstat on Microsoft operating systems, but we can also put Nmap to use for such tasks.

As we discussed in Chapter 8, Nmap can allow us to discover the devices on our networks, but it can also allow us to determine on which network ports a given system is listening. If we run the following Nmap command:

Nmap < IP address >

we will see results similar to those shown in Figure 9.2.

In this case, we can immediately point out several common services running on the target:

- **Port 22** Remote access to the system, secured with Secure Shell (SSH)
- **Port 53** Domain name system (DNS), which translates friendly names to IP addresses
- **Port 80** Hypertext Transfer Protocol (HTTP), which serves Web content
- **Port 443** Hypertext Transfer Protocol Secure (HTTPS), which serves Web pages secured with Secure Sockets Layer (SSL) and/or Transport Layer Security (TLS)

Several other ports are open as well, running various services. We can use this information as a starting place for closing down undesirable services. In the case of our example target, ports 22, 80, and 443 being open might be notable if we did not intend to allow remote access or serve Web content.

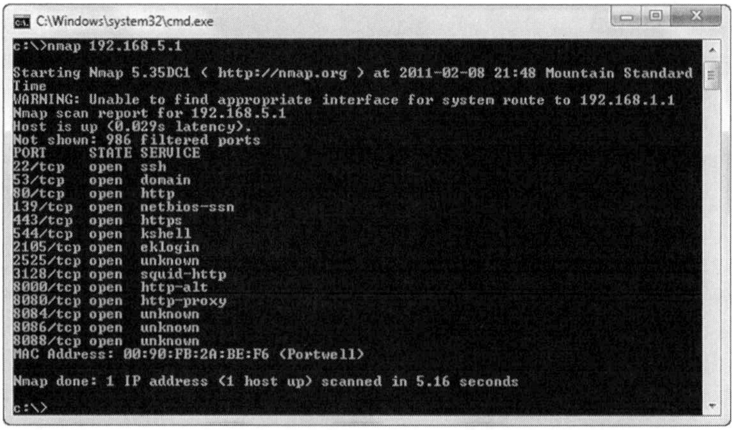

FIGURE 9.2
Nmap Scan Result

Alter Default Accounts

A common weakness in many operating systems is the use of accounts known to be standard. In many operating systems, we can find the equivalent of a guest account and an administrator account. We may also find a variety of others, including those intended for the use of support personnel, to allow services or utilities to operate, and a plethora of others, widely varying by the operating system vendor, version, and so forth. Such accounts are commonly referred to as default accounts.

In some cases, the default accounts may come equipped with excessively liberal permissions to regulate the actions they are allowed to carry out, which can cause a great deal of trouble when they are being used by an informed attacker. We may also find that default accounts are set with a particular password or no password at all. If we allow such accounts to remain on the system with their default settings, we may be leaving the proverbial doors that protect access to our system wide open so that attackers can simply stroll right in and make themselves at home.

Typical measures we would take to mitigate such security risks are generally very simple to carry out. We should first decide whether the accounts are needed at all, and disable or remove any we will not be using. In the case of guest accounts, support accounts, and others of a similar nature, we can often quickly and easily turn the accounts off or remove them entirely without causing problems for ourselves. In the case of administrative accounts, often with names such as administrator, admin, or root, we may not be able to safely remove them from the system, or the operating system may prevent us from doing so. In most cases, however, such accounts can be renamed in order to confound attackers who might attempt to make use of them. Lastly, we should not leave any account with a default password, no matter what its status, as such passwords are often documented and well known.

Apply the Principle of Least Privilege

As we discussed in Chapter 3, the principle of least privilege dictates that we only allow a party the absolute minimum permission needed for it to carry out its function. Depending on the operating system in question, we may find this idea put into practice to a greater or a lesser extent. In almost any modern operating system, we can find the tasks a particular user is allowed to carry out separated into those that require administrative privileges and those that do not.

In general, normal operating system users are allowed to read and write files, and perhaps execute scripts or programs, but they are limited to doing so within a certain restricted portion of the file system. Normal users are generally not allowed to carry out tasks such as modifying the way hardware functions, making changes to the files on which the operating system itself depends, installing software that can change or affect the entire operating system, and so on. Such activities are generally restricted to those users that are allowed administrative access.

On most UNIX and Linux-like operating systems, we can often see such roles strictly enforced. Although it would be possible for the administrator of such a system to allow all users to act with the privileges of an administrator, this is generally not the convention and administrative or "root" access is often guarded carefully. On Microsoft operating systems, we can often find the exact opposite to be true. On a Windows operating system, we may find that the majority of the users allowed to log directly into the operating system are given administrative rights. Although there are no technical reasons for such common differences in the privileges given to user accounts between the two operating systems, there is generally a difference in the mindset of the users and administrators who configure such accounts.

When we allow the average system user to regularly function with administrative privileges, we leave ourselves open to a wide array of security issues. If the user executes a malware-infected file or application, he does so as the administrator and that program has considerably more freedom to alter the operating system and other software installed on the host. If an attacker compromises a user's account, and that account has been given administrative rights, we have now given the keys to the entire system directly to the attacker. Nearly any type of attack we might discuss, launched from nearly any source, will have considerably more impact when allowed access to administrative rights on a host.

If, instead, we limit the privileges on our systems to the minimum needed in order to allow our users to perform their required tasks, we go a long way toward mitigating many security issues. In many cases, attacks will fail entirely when an attacker attempts to run them from a user account running with a limited set of permissions. This is a very cheap and easy security measure we can put in place, and is simple to implement.

Perform Updates

Regular and timely updates to our operating systems and applications are critical to maintaining strong security. New attacks are published on a regular basis, and if we do not apply the security patches released by the vendors that manufacture our operating systems and applications, we will likely fall victim very quickly to a large number of well-known attacks.

We can look to the various items of malware propagating over the Internet at any given time as an excellent example of this idea. Many pieces of malware are able to spread by exploiting known vulnerabilities that have long since been patched by the software vendors. Although it does pay to be prudent when planning to install software updates and to test them thoroughly before doing so, it is generally unwise to delay this process for very long.

One of the most crucial times to ensure that we have properly patched a system is directly after we have finished installing it. If we connect a newly installed and completely unpatched system to our network, we may see it attacked and compromised in very short order, even on internal networks. The commonly considered best practice in such a situation is to download the patches onto removable media and use this media to patch the system before ever connecting it to a network.

Turn On Logging and Auditing

Last, but certainly not least, we should configure and turn on the appropriate logging and auditing features for our system. Although the particulars of how we configure such services may vary slightly depending on the operating system in question, and the use to which the system is to be put, we generally need to be able to keep an accurate and complete record of the important processes and activities that take place on our systems. We will generally want to log significant events such as the exercise of administrative privileges, users logging in to and out of the system, or failing to log in, changes made to the operating system, and a number of similar activities taking place.

Depending on the environment into which we will be placing the system, we may also want to include additional features to supplement the tools built into the operating system for these purposes. We may want to install a variety of monitoring tools that watch the functionality of the system and alert us to issues with the system itself or anomalies that might show in the various system or application logs. We might also want to install supplementary logging architecture in order to monitor the activities of multiple machines, or to simply allow duplicate remote copies of logs to be maintained outside the system to help ensure that we have an unaltered record of the activities that might have taken place on the system.

It is also important to note that actually reviewing the logs is a vital part of the process. If we collect logs but never review them, we might as well not collect them at all.

PROTECTING AGAINST MALWARE

A large concern at present is the mind-boggling number and variety of malware present on the networks, systems, and storage devices around the globe. Using such tools, attackers can disable systems, steal data, conduct social engineering attacks, blackmail users, gather intelligence, and perform a number of other attacks.

At the time of this writing, we have a good example of a particularly complex and impactful item of malware to examine in Stuxnet. Stuxnet was first discovered in July 2009, albeit in a somewhat weaker form than what it ultimately reached [2]. Although the number of systems infected with it was much lower in comparison to some of the other major malware outbreaks that have taken place over the years, it had a much more specific focus in that it targeted the Supervisory Control and Data Acquisition (SCADA) systems that run various industrial processes.

ADDITIONAL RESOURCES

For considerably more detail on what Stuxnet does and how it does it, see the "W32. Stuxnet Dossier" from Symantec, available at www.symantec.com/content/en/us/ enterprise/media/security_response/whitepapers/w32_stuxnet_dossier.pdf.

The ultimate goal of Stuxnet appears to have been the sabotage of SCADA systems, largely targeted at portions of the equipment running in the nuclear program in Iran [3]. Stuxnet has raised the bar for malware from largely being an annoyance to actually being physically destructive.

Anti-Malware Tools

Most anti-malware applications detect threats in the same way the IDSes we discussed in Chapter 8 do: either by matching against a signature or by detecting anomalous activities taking place. Anti-malware tools do tend to depend more heavily on signatures than on anomaly detection, which is typically referred to in the anti-malware field as heuristics. Malware signatures are usually updated by the vendor of the application at least once a day and may be updated more often than that if the need arises.

Anti-malware tools generally detect malware in one of two main ways: either by detecting the presence of, or traffic indicative of, malware in real time, or by performing scans of the files and processes already in place on the system. When malware is found, responses by the anti-malware tool may include killing any associated processes and deleting the files, killing the processes and quarantining the files so that they are not able to execute but are not deleted, or simply leaving whatever has been detected alone. Leaving the files intact is not a typical response, but may be required as anti-malware tools do sometimes detect security tools and other files that are not malware, which we may want to leave alone and ignore in the future.

We can find anti-malware tools deployed on individual systems and a variety of servers as a matter of course for enterprise environments in order to protect these systems. We may also find such tools installed on proxy servers in order to filter malware out of the incoming and outgoing traffic. This is very common in the case of proxies for e-mail, as many items of malware use e-mail as a method of propagation. In the case where malware is detected by such a tool, we may see the e-mail rejected entirely, or we may merely see the malware stripped out of the message body or the offending attachment removed.

Executable Space Protection

Executable space protection is a hardware- and software-based technology that can be implemented by operating systems in order to foil attacks that use the same techniques we commonly see used in malware. In short, executable space protection prevents certain portions of the memory used by the operating system and applications from being used to execute code. This means classic attacks such as buffer overflows that depend on being able to execute their commands in hijacked portions of memory may be prevented from functioning at all. Many operating systems also use address space layout randomization (ASLR) [4] in order to shift the contents of the memory in use around so that tampering with it is even more difficult.

MORE ADVANCED

A buffer overflow attack works by inputting more data than an application is expecting from a particular input—for example, by entering 1,000 characters into a field that was only expecting 10. Depending on how the application was written, we may find that the extra 990 characters are written somewhere into memory, perhaps over memory locations used by other applications or the operating system. It is sometimes possible to execute commands by specifically crafting the excess data.

Executable space protection requires two components to function: a hardware component and a software component. Both of the main CPU chip manufacturers, Intel and AMD, support executable space protection, with Intel calling it the Execute Disable (XD) bit [5] and AMD calling it Enhanced Virus Protection [6].

The software implementation of executable space prevention can be found in many common operating systems. Both executable space prevention and ASLR can be found in many operating systems from Microsoft and Apple, as well as a number of Linux distributions, just to name a few.

SOFTWARE FIREWALLS AND HOST INTRUSION DETECTION

In addition to the tools we can use on the network to detect and filter out undesirable traffic, such as firewalls and IDSes, we can add another layer of security at the host level by implementing a very similar set of tools here. Although we may often find firewalls and IDSes implemented at the network level in the form of purpose-built appliances, the actual functions they perform are generally carried out via specialized software resident on the devices. Similar software can be installed directly onto the hosts residing on our networks.

Software Firewalls

Properly configured software firewalls are a very useful additional layer of security we can add to the hosts residing on our networks. Such firewalls generally contain a subset of the features we might find on a large firewall appliance but are often capable of very similar packet filtering and stateful packet inspection. We often find the rulesets of such applications expressed in terms of the particular applications and ports allowed to send and receive traffic on the various network interfaces that exist on the host. Such softwares can range from the relatively simple versions that are built into and ship with common operating systems, such as Windows and OS X, to large versions intended for use on corporate networks that include centralized monitoring and the capability for considerably more complex rules and management options.

Host Intrusion Detection

Host-based intrusion detection systems (HIDSes) are used to analyze the activities on or directed at the network interface of a particular host. They have many of the same advantages as network-based intrusion detection systems (NIDSes) have but with a considerably reduced scope of operation. As with software firewalls, such tools may range from simple consumer versions to much more complex commercial versions that allow for centralized monitoring and management.

A potential flaw with centrally managed HIDSes is that, in order for the software to report an attack to the management mechanism in real time, the information needs to be communicated over the network. If the host in question is being actively attacked via the same network we would report over, we may not be able to do this. We can attempt to mitigate such issues by sending a regular beacon from the device to the management mechanism, allowing us to assume a problem if we stop seeing multiple devices unexpectedly, but this might not be a complete approach.

OPERATING SYSTEM SECURITY TOOLS

As we discussed in our coverage of the tools we might use to evaluate our network security in Chapter 8, a number of the same or similar tools can also be used to assess the security of our hosts. We can use scanners to examine how our hosts interact with the rest of the devices on the network, vulnerability assessment tools to help point out particular areas where we might find applications or services that may be open to attack, privilege escalation tools to gain unauthorized access on our systems, and various exploit frameworks to allow us access to a broad array of tools and attacks that might be used by those who would attempt to subvert our security. The tools we will discuss in this section do not resemble an exhaustive list, but we will hit a few of the highlights.

Scanners

We can use a large number of scanning tools to assist in detecting various security flaws when we are looking at hosts. Although we discussed this in Chapter 8 from a network perspective, such tools can also be used to enhance the security of our hosts. We can look for open ports and versions of services that are running, examine banners displayed by services for information, examine the information our systems display over the network, and perform a large number of similar tasks.

Earlier in this chapter, when we were discussing hardening, we looked at a very simple example of using Nmap to look at a device over the network in order to discover the ports that had services listening on them. Nmap actually has a very large and broad set of functionality and can give us considerably more information if we ask it to do so. In Figure 9.3, we can see the results of an Nmap scan directed against a network printer. In this case, we asked Nmap to also look for the particular versions of the services it found, and to attempt to identify the operating system running on the device. If we look at port 9220 in the listing, we can see that the service is hp-gsg, which, although a bit cryptic, might give us somewhat of a clue that it is a service specific to HP printers, but if we look at the version information on the same line, we can see very specifically that the service is HP Generic Scan Gateway 1.0. Based on this information, we might have a much better chance of successfully being able to attack the device.

ALERT!

Looking closer at the Nmap results in Figure 9.3, you will notice that Nmap told us the device being scanned was a printer, but it also told us it was running Mac OS X as an operating system. Sometimes Nmap's OS fingerprints can be a little skewed from what is actually on the device, so it is often best to verify the output from Nmap with another tool if something looks odd.

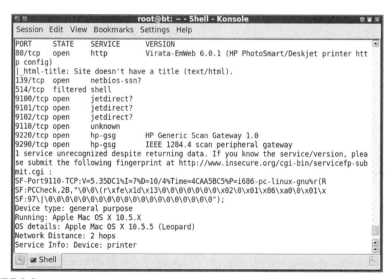

FIGURE 9.3
Nmap Scan Result

In addition to the many features built into Nmap, we can create custom Nmap functionality of our own, through the use of the Nmap Scripting Engine (NSE).

Vulnerability Assessment Tools

Vulnerability assessment tools, which often include some portion of the feature set we might find in a tool such as Nmap, are aimed specifically at the task of finding and reporting network services on hosts that have known vulnerabilities.

One such well-known scanning tool is Tenable's Nessus. Although Nessus was, at one time, a free tool, it is no longer entirely so. Nessus is now primarily a commercial tool, with a limited free license available for noncommercial use. Nessus is chiefly a graphically interfaced vulnerability assessment tool, as shown in Figure 9.4. In essence, Nessus will conduct a port scan on a target, then attempt to determine what services and versions of service are running on any ports it finds open. Nessus will then report back with a specific list of vulnerabilities that we might find on a given device.

As we mentioned, Nessus, as a part of its feature set, includes a port scanner, as a port scan is needed in order to find the listening services before we can identify the vulnerabilities that might be resident in them. Nessus also includes some other functionality, including the ability to add custom features to the tool through the Nessus Attack Scripting Language (NASL).

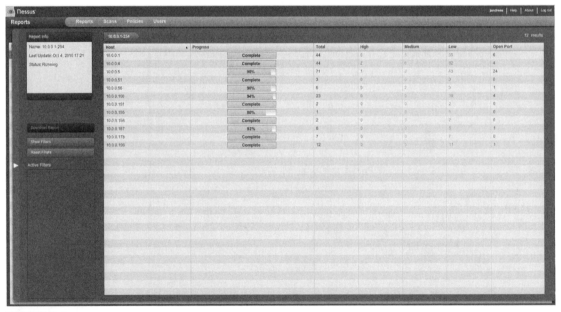

FIGURE 9.4
Nessus

Exploit Frameworks

A category of tools, or more accurately, a category of sets of tools, called an exploit framework, enjoyed a rise in popularity in the first few years of the 2000s and is still going strong. Many exploit frameworks provide a variety of tools, including network mapping tools, sniffers, and many more, but one of the main tools we can find in exploit frameworks is, logically, the exploit.

Exploits are small bits of software that take advantage of, or exploit, flaws in other software or applications in order to cause them to behave in ways that were not intended by their creators. Exploits are commonly used by attackers to gain access to systems or gain additional privileges on them when they already have access.

Exploit frameworks, such as Rapid7's Metasploit, as shown in Figure 9.5, Immunity CANVAS, and Core Impact, provide large sets of prepackaged exploits in order to make them simple to use and to make a larger library available to us than we might have if we had to put them together individually. Many exploit frameworks come in the form of graphically interfaced tools that can be run in much the same way that any other application functions. Some tools can even be configured to automatically seek out and attack systems, spreading further into the network as they gain additional access.

FIGURE 9.5
Metasploit Pro

OPERATING SYSTEM SECURITY IN THE REAL WORLD

The operating system security measures we discussed in this chapter are in common use in companies around the globe. The various steps we went over when we discussed hardening operating systems are usually implemented by any competent organization that is building servers for deployment, particularly in cases where these servers will be Internet facing. Depending on the organization in question and its security posture, we may or may not find such measures to have been carried out on client machines. Although such basic hardening measures are a way in which we can increase our security with relative ease, we do so at the potential expense of ease of use and productivity.

The use of anti-malware tools, HIDSes, and software firewalls is also rather ubiquitous in many organizations of any appreciable size. We will commonly see anti-malware tools installed on proxy servers filtering Web and mail traffic as it enters from the Internet. Without such tools in place, even if we have very strong border security in the form of firewalls and IDSes, when something does manage to make it through these measures it will cause great havoc on our internal networks.

The tools we discussed in this chapter and in Chapter 8 are some of the staples of the security industry. A huge number and variety of such tools might be used in any given environment for any number of uses, but taking the time to learn some of those that are more commonly seen, such as Nmap and Nessus, will be helpful to anyone entering the security field. We may see larger and costlier commercial tools at use in a given environment, but they will often be in use side by side with the old standbys.

SUMMARY

One of the primary tools we can use in our efforts to secure the operating systems for which we are responsible is hardening. The main tasks, when we seek to harden an operating system, are to remove all unnecessary software, remove all unessential services, alter the default accounts on the system, utilize the principle of least privilege, apply updates to software in an appropriate manner, and conduct logging and auditing.

We can also apply various additional layers of security to our operating systems in the form of additional software. We can install anti-malware tools in an effort to detect, prevent, and remove malware when we encounter it. We can put firewall technology to use directly on our hosts, in order to filter out undesirable traffic as it enters or exits our network interfaces. We can also install HIDSes in order to detect attacks as they come at us over the network.

In our efforts to secure our operating systems, we can make use of a variety of security tools in order to find the security flaws that might be present. A number of scanning tools are available, with Nmap being one of the most well known among them. We can also make use of vulnerability assessment tools in order to locate specific security flaws in our services or network-enabled software, such as Nessus. Additionally, we can use exploit frameworks to attack systems in an effort to gain access to them or to gain elevated privilege levels, with Metasploit being one of the better-known tools.

EXERCISES

1. What is a vector for malware propagation?
2. What is an exploit framework?
3. What is the difference between a port scanner and a vulnerability assessment tool?
4. Explain the concept of an attack surface.

5. Why might we want a firewall on our host if one already exists on the network?
6. What is operating system hardening?
7. What is the XD bit and why do we use it?
8. What does executable space protection do for us?
9. How does the principle of least privilege apply to operating system hardening?
10. Download Nmap from www.nmap.org and install it. Conduct a basic scan of scanme.nmap.org using either the Zenmap GUI or the command line. What ports can you find open?

Bibliography

[1] F.B. Schneider, (Ed.), Trust in Cyberspace, National Academy Press, Washington, D.C., 1998 ISBN-13: 9780309065580.

[2] N. Falliere, L.O. Murchu, E. Chien, W32.Stuxnet Dossier, Symantec, 2011.

[3] Ed Barnes, Mystery surrounds cyber missile that crippled Iran's nuclear weapons ambitions, Fox News. <www.foxnews.com/scitech/2010/11/26/secret-agent-crippled-irans-nuclear-ambitions/>, November 26, 2010 (cited: February 13, 2011).

[4] E.G. Barrantes, D.H. Ackley, T.S. Palmer, D.D. Zovi, S. Forrest, D. Stefanovic, Randomized instruction setemulation to disrupt binary code injection attacks, Proceedings of the 10th ACM Conference on Computer and Communications Security, 2003. ISBN: 1581137389.

[5] Intel Corporation, Execute disable bit and enterprise security, Intel.com. <www.intel.com/technology/xdbit/index.htm>, 2011 (cited: February 13, 2011).

[6] Advanced Micro Devices, Inc. Enhanced virus protection, AMD.com. <www.amd.com/us/products/technologies/enhanced-virus-protection/Pages/enhanced-virus-protection.aspx>, 2011 (cited: February 13, 2011).

CHAPTER 10

Application Security

Information in This Chapter:

- Software Development Vulnerabilities
- Web Security
- Database Security
- Application Security Tools

INTRODUCTION

In Chapters 8 and 9, we discussed the need to keep our networks and operating systems secure from the variety of attacks and incidents that might befall them. Equally important to ensuring that we can keep attackers from interacting with our networks in an unauthorized manner and subverting our operating system security is ensuring that our applications are not misused.

As a good illustration of the importance of all three realms of security, we can look to any of the nearly constant streams of security breaches that take place in companies around the globe. One particular incident that was wide reaching in terms of the methods used in the attack was the TJX breach.

The TJX Breach

The TJX Companies, a retailer operating more than 2,000 stores under the brands T.J. Maxx, Marshalls, Winners, Homesense, T.K. Maxx, HomeGoods, A.J. Wright, and Bob's Stores, reported a breach of financial data in January 2007. It was later announced that data regarding sales transactions for 2003, as well as May through December 2006, had been exposed, with an estimated total of 45 million to 200 million debit and credit card numbers having been stolen, as well as 455,000 records containing identification information, names, and addresses.

The very beginning of the breach was an attack on the wireless network used to communicate between handheld price-checking devices, cash registers, and the store's computers, at a Marshalls retail store in Minnesota [1]. The system used the 802.11b wireless protocol to communicate and Wired Equivalent Privacy (WEP) encryption to secure the transmission media. WEP is an outdated encryption protocol with well-known weaknesses and was rendered obsolete in 2002 [2].

Once the attackers gained access to the system at a local store, they were able to access the central system at the parent company, TJX, in Massachusetts. Once in the system, the attackers were able to create their own accounts and access the stolen data directly from the Internet. This was possible due to the lack of firewalls and encryption on sensitive portions of the TJX network [3].

In the breach outlined in the preceding case study, we can clearly see examples of network security issues and operating system security issues, both of which are relatively common when we look at security breaches. One of the things that makes the attack sting the most from a security perspective is that the attackers were able to turn TJX's own systems against itself in order to gain access to sensitive data, by using the normal channels within the company in an unauthorized manner. If we do not protect our applications, we are potentially missing a critical portion of the attack surface that needs to be secured.

SOFTWARE DEVELOPMENT VULNERABILITIES

A number of common software development vulnerabilities can lead to security issues in our applications. These issues are all well known as being problematic from a security perspective, and the reasons the development practices that lead to them should not be used are a frequent topic of discussion in both the information security and software engineering communities.

The main categories of software development vulnerabilities include buffer overflows, race conditions, input validation attacks, authentication attacks, authorization attacks, and cryptographic attacks, as shown in Figure 10.1. All these vulnerabilities can be avoided with relative ease when developing new software by simply not using the particular programming techniques that enable them to exist.

ADDITIONAL RESOURCES

A great resource for secure software development standards is the set of documentation available from the Computer Emergency Response Team (CERT) at Carnegie Mellon University.[1] This organization provides secure coding documentation for several programming languages and is a good overall resource for further investigation into secure coding in general.

---

[1] www.cert.org/cert/information/developers.html.

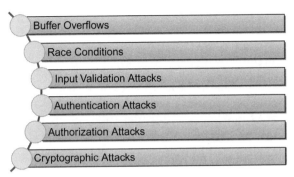

FIGURE 10.1
Main Software Development Vulnerabilities

Buffer Overflows

Buffer overflows, also referred to as buffer overruns, occur when we do not properly account for the size of the data input into our applications. If we are taking data into an application, most programming languages will require that we specify the amount of data we expect to receive, and set aside storage for that data. If we do not set a limit on the amount of data we take in, called bounds checking, we may receive 1,000 characters of input where we had only allocated storage for 50 characters.

In this case, the excess 950 characters of data may be written over other areas in memory that are in use by other applications, or by the operating system itself. An attacker might use this technique to allow him to tamper with other applications, or to cause the operating system to execute his own commands.

Proper bounds checking can nullify this type of attack entirely. Depending on the language we choose for the development effort, bounds checking may be implemented automatically, as is the case with Java and C# [4].

Race Conditions

Race conditions occur when multiple processes or multiple threads within a process control or share access to a particular resource, and the correct handling of that resource depends on the proper ordering or timing of transactions.

For example, if we are making a $20 withdrawal from our bank account via an ATM, the process might go as follows:

1. Check the account balance ($100)
2. Withdraw funds ($20)
3. Update the account balance ($80)

If someone else starts the same process at roughly the same time and tries to make a $30 withdrawal, we might end up with a bit of a problem:

1. User 1: Check the account balance ($100)
2. User 2: Check the account balance ($100)

3. User 1: Withdraw funds ($20)
4. User 2: Withdraw funds ($30)
5. User 1: Update the account balance ($80)
6. User 2: Update the account balance ($70)

Because access to the resource, our bank account, is shared, we end up with a balance of $70 being recorded, where we should see only $50. In reality, our bank will have implemented measures to keep this from happening, but this illustrates the idea of a race condition. Our two users "race" to access the resource, and undesirable conditions occur.

Race conditions can be very difficult to detect in existing software, as they are hard to reproduce. When we are developing new applications, careful handling of the way we access resources to avoid dependencies on timing can generally avoid such issues.

Input Validation Attacks

If we are not careful to validate the input to our applications, we may find ourselves on the bad side of a number of issues, depending on the particular environment and language being used. A good example of an input validation problem is the format string attack.

Format string attacks are an issue where certain print functions within a programming language can be used to manipulate or view the internal memory of an application. In some languages, C and C + + in particular, we can insert certain characters into our commands that will apply formatting to the data we are printing to the screen, such as %f, %n, %p, and so on. Although such parameters are indeed a legitimate part of the language, if we are not careful to filter the data input into our applications, they can also be used to attack us.

For example, if an attacker were to include the %n (write an integer into memory) parameter in an input field and had specifically crafted the rest of the input, he or she might be able to write a particular value into a location in memory that might not normally be accessible to him or her. The attacker could use this technique to crash an application or cause the operating system to run a command, potentially allowing him or her to compromise the system.

This type of attack is almost entirely one of input validation. If we are careful to check the input we are taking in, and filter it for unexpected or undesirable content, we can often halt any issues immediately. In the case of the format string attack, we may be able to remove the offending characters from the input, or put error handling in place to ensure that they do not cause a problem.

Authentication Attacks

When we plan the authentication mechanisms our applications will use, taking care to use strong mechanisms will help to ensure that we can react in a reasonable manner in the face of attacks. There are a number of common factors across the various mechanisms we might choose that will help make them stronger.

If we put a requirement for strong passwords into our applications when we are doing password authentication, this will go a long way toward helping to keep attackers out. If we use an eight-character, all-lowercase password, such as *hellobob*, a reasonably powerful machine may be able to break the password in a matter of seconds. If we use an eight-character, mixed-case password that also includes a number and a symbol, such as *H3lloBob!*, our time goes up to more than two years [5]. Furthermore, our applications should not use passwords that are built-in and are not changeable, often referred to as hard-coded passwords.

Additionally, performing any authentication steps on the client side is generally not a good idea, as we then place such measures where they may easily be attacked. As a good example of why we should not do client-side authentication, we can look to the incident involving certain hardware-encrypted flash drives from SanDisk, Kingston, and Verbatim that was reported in January 2010 [6]. In this case, it was found that an application running on the user's computer was responsible for verifying that the decryption password entered was actually correct, and sent a fixed code to the device to unlock it. Security researchers were able to build a tool to send the same unlock code without needing the password and were able to circumvent the security of the devices entirely [7].

Authorization Attacks

Just as we discussed when we looked at authentication, placing authorization mechanisms on the client side is a bad idea as well. Any such process that is performed in a space where it might be subject to direct attack or manipulation by users is almost guaranteed to be a security issue at some point. We should instead authenticate against a remote server, or on the hardware of the device, if we have a portable device, where we are considerably more in control.

When we are authorizing a user for some activity, we should do so using the principle of least privilege, as we discussed in Chapter 3. If we are not careful to allow the minimum permissions required, both for our users and for the internal activities of our software, we may leave ourselves open for attack and compromise.

Additionally, whenever a user or process attempts an activity that requires particular privileges, we should always check again to ensure that the user is indeed authorized for the activity in question, each time it is attempted. If we have a user who, whether by accident or by design, gains access to restricted portions of our application, we should have measures in place that will not allow the user to proceed.

Cryptographic Attacks

We leave ourselves open to failure if we do not pay close enough attention to designing our security mechanisms while we implement cryptographic controls in our applications. Cryptography is easy to implement badly, and this can give us a false sense of security.

One of the big "gotchas" in implementing cryptography is to give in to the temptation to develop a cryptographic scheme of our own devising. The major cryptographic algorithms in use today, such as Advanced Encryption Standard (AES) and RSA, have been developed and tested by thousands of people who are very skilled and make their living developing such tools. Additionally, such algorithms are in general use because they have been able to stand the test of time without serious compromise. Although it is possible that our homegrown algorithm may have something to offer, software that stores or processes any sort of sensitive data is likely not a good place to test it out.

In addition to using known algorithms, we should also plan for the mechanisms we do select to become obsolete or compromised in the future. This means, in our software design, we should allow for the use of different algorithms, or at least design our applications in such a way that changing them is not a Herculean task. We should also plan for changing the encryption keys the software uses, in case our keys break or become exposed.

WEB SECURITY

As the use of Web pages and applications has become prevalent in recent years, careful design and development of them is paramount. Attackers can use an enormous variety of techniques to compromise our machines, steal sensitive information, and trick us into carrying out activities without our knowledge. These types of attacks divide into two main categories: client-side attacks and server-side attacks.

Client-Side Attacks

Client-side attacks take advantage of weaknesses in the software loaded on our clients, or those attacks that use social engineering to trick us into going along with the attack. There are a large number of such attacks, but we will focus specifically on some that use the Web as an attack vehicle.

CROSS-SITE SCRIPTING

Cross-site scripting (XSS) is an attack carried out by placing code in the form of a scripting language into a Web page, or other media, that is interpreted by a client browser, including Adobe Flash animation and some types of video files. When another person views the Web page or media, he or she executes the code automatically, and the attack is carried out. A good example of such an attack might be for the attacker to leave a comment containing the attack script in the comments section of an entry on a blog. Every person reading the command in her browser would execute the attack.

ALERT!

As we discussed, cross-site scripting is abbreviated as XSS, which may be a bit confusing to some. This was done because the acronym CSS was already used for Cascading Style Sheets, another Web-related technology.

CROSS-SITE REQUEST FORGERY

A cross-site request forgery (XSRF) attack is similar to XSS, in a general sense. In this type of attack, the attacker places a link, or links, on a Web page in such a way that they will be automatically executed, in order to initiate a particular activity on another Web page or application where the user is currently authenticated. For instance, such a link might cause the browser to add items to our shopping cart on Amazon, or transfer money from one bank account to another.

If we are browsing several pages and are still authenticated to the same page the attack is intended for, we might execute the attack in the background and never know it. For example, if we have several pages open in our browser, including one for MySpiffyBank.com, a common banking institution, and we are still logged in to that page when we visit BadGuyAttackSite.com, the links on the attack page may automatically execute in order to get us to transfer money to another account.

This type of attack takes somewhat of a shotgun approach in order to be carried out successfully. The attacker will most likely not know which Web sites the user is authenticated to but can guess at some of the more common choices, such as banks or shopping sites, and include components to target those specifically.

CLICKJACKING

Clickjacking is an attack that takes advantage of the graphical display capabilities of our browser to trick us into clicking on something we might not otherwise. Clickjacking attacks work by placing another layer over the page, or portions of the page, in order to obscure what we are actually clicking. For example, the attacker might hide a button that says "buy now" under another layer with a button that says "more information."

DEFENSE

These types of attacks are, for the most part, thwarted by the newer versions of the common browsers, such as Internet Explorer, Firefox, Safari, and Chrome. The most common attacks we discussed in this section will be blocked by these automatically, but the landscape of attacks is constantly changing. In many cases, however, new attack vectors are simply variations of old attacks. Additionally, there are innumerable vulnerable clients running on outdated or unpatched software that are still vulnerable to attacks that are years old.

Understanding how the common attacks work and protecting against them not only gives us an additional measure of security but also helps us understand how newer attacks might be developed.

It is very important to keep up with the most recent browser versions and updates, as the vendors that produce them regularly update their protections. Furthermore, for some browsers, we can apply additional tools in order to protect us from client-side attacks. One of the better known of these tools is NoScript[2] and is presently only available for Firefox. NoScript blocks most Web page scripts by default and allows only those that we specifically enable. With careful use, script-blocking tools such as this can disable many of the Web-based threats we might encounter.

Server-Side Attacks

On the server side of the Web transaction, a number of vulnerabilities may cause us problems as well. Such threats and vulnerabilities can vary widely depending on our operating system, Web server software, various software versions, scripting languages, and many other factors. Across all of these, however, are several factors that are the cause of numerous security issues that are common across the various implementations we might encounter.

LACK OF INPUT VALIDATION

Lack of proper input validation is a large problem when we look at Web platforms. As we discussed earlier in the chapter, this is a general security issue when developing software, but some of the most common server-side Web attacks use this weakness to carry out their attacks.

SQL injection gives us a strong example of what might happen if we do not properly validate the input of our Web applications. Structured Query Language (SQL) is the language we use to communicate with many of the common databases on the market today. In the case of databases connected to Web applications, entering specially crafted data into the Web forms that interact with them can sometimes produce results not anticipated by the application developers. We will discuss the specifics of SQL injection in more depth later in this chapter.

If we are careful to validate the input we take into our Web applications, and filter out characters that might be used to compromise our security, we can often fend off such an attack before it even begins. In many cases, filtering out special characters such as *, %, ', ;, and / will defeat such attacks entirely.

IMPROPER OR INADEQUATE PERMISSIONS

Inadequate permissions can often cause us problems with Web applications, and Internet-facing applications of most any kind. Particularly with Web applications and pages, there are often sensitive files and directories that will cause

---

[2] http://noscript.net/.

security issues if they are exposed to general users. One area that might cause us trouble is the exposure of configuration files.

For example, in many Web applications that make use of a database (that is a vast majority of them), there are configuration files that hold the credentials the application uses to access the database. If these files and the directories that hold them are not properly secured, an attacker may simply read our credentials from the file and access the database as he or she pleases. For applications that hold sensitive data, this could be disastrous.

Likewise, for the directories on our Web servers, if we do not take care to secure them properly, this may be pointed out to us in a less than desirable way. We may find files changed in our applications, new files added, or the contents deleted entirely. Unsecure applications that are Internet facing do not tend to last very long before being compromised.

EXTRANEOUS FILES

When we move a Web server from development into production, one of the tasks often missed in the process is that of cleaning up any files not directly related to running the site or application, or that might be artifacts of the development or build process.

If we leave archives of the source code from which our applications are built, backup copies of our files, text files containing our notes or credentials, or any such related files, we may be handing an attacker exactly the materials he or she needs in order to compromise our system. One of the final steps when we are rolling out such a server should be to make sure all such files are cleaned up, or moved elsewhere if they are still needed. This is also a good periodic check to ensure that, in the course of troubleshooting or upgrading, these items have not been left behind where they are visible to the general public.

DATABASE SECURITY

As we discussed when we went over Web security issues, the vast majority of Web sites and applications in use today make use of databases in order to store the information they display and process. In some cases, such applications may hold very sensitive data, such as tax returns, medical data, or legal records; or they may contain only the contents of a discussion forum on knitting. In either case, the data such applications hold is important to the owners of the application and they would be inconvenienced, at the very least, if it were damaged or manipulated in an unauthorized manner.

A number of issues can cause trouble in ensuring the security of our databases. The canonical list includes the following [8]:

- Unauthenticated flaws in network protocols
- Authenticated flaws in network protocols
- Flaws in authentication protocols
- Unauthenticated access to functionality

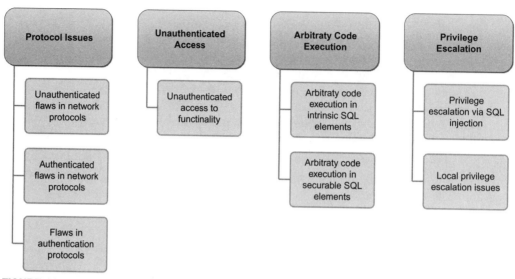

FIGURE 10.2
Categories of Database Security Issues

- Arbitrary code execution in intrinsic SQL elements
- Arbitrary code execution in securable SQL elements
- Privilege escalation via SQL injection
- Local privilege escalation issues

Although this may seem like a horribly complex set of issues for us to worry about, we can break them down into four major categories, as shown in Figure 10.2.

Protocol Issues

We might find a number of issues in the protocols in use by any given database. We can look at the network protocols used to communicate with the database, some of which will need a set of credentials in order to use and some of which will not. In either case, there is often a steady stream of vulnerabilities for most any major database product and version we might care to examine. Such vulnerabilities often involve some of the more common software development issues, such as the buffer overflows we discussed at the beginning of this chapter.

When we are dealing with known protocol issues, the absolute best defense is to ensure that we are using the most current software version and patches for the database software in question, as we discussed in Chapter 9. Defending against presently unknown network protocol issues often revolves around limiting access to our databases, either in the sense of actually limiting access to who is able to connect to the database over the network, using some of the methods we discussed in Chapter 8, or, in the case of authenticated protocol problems, by limiting the privileges and accounts we make available for the database itself, following the principle of least privilege.

We may also have issues in the authentication protocols used by our database, depending on the specific software and version we have in use. In general, the older and more out-of-date our software becomes, the more likely it is that we are using an authentication protocol that is not robust. Many older applications will use authentication protocols we know to have been broken at some point, or to have obvious architectural flaws, such as sending login credentials over the network in plaintext (refer to Chapter 5), as Telnet does. Again, the best defense here is to ensure that we are on current versions of the software we are using.

Unauthenticated Access

When we give a user or process the opportunity to interact with our database without supplying a set of credentials, we create the possibility for security issues. Such issues may be related to simple queries to the database through a Web interface, in which we might accidentally expose information contained in the database; or we might expose information on the database itself, such as a version number, giving an attacker additional material with which to compromise our application.

We might also experience a wide variety of issues related to the secure software development practices we discussed at the beginning of the chapter. If the user or process is forced to send us a set of credentials to begin a transaction, we can monitor, or place limits on, what the user or process is allowed to do, based on those credentials. If we allow access to part of our application or tool set without requiring these credentials, we may lose visibility and control over what actions are taking place.

Arbitrary Code Execution

We can find a number of areas for security flaws in the languages we use to talk to databases. Generally, these are concentrated on SQL, as it is the most common database language in use. In the default SQL language, a number of built-in elements are possible security risks, some of which we can control access to and some of which we cannot.

In these language elements, we may find a number of issues related to bugs in the software we are using, or issues spawned by not using secure coding practices, that might allow us to execute arbitrary code within the application. For example, a flaw allowing us to conduct a buffer overflow, as we discussed earlier in this chapter, might enable us to insert attack code into the memory space used by the database or the operating system, and compromise either or both of them.

Our best defenses against such attacks are twofold. From the consumer side, we should stay current on the version and patch levels for our software. From the vendor side, we should mandate secure coding practices, in all cases, in order to eliminate the vulnerabilities in the first place, as well as conducting internal reviews to ensure that such practices are actually being followed.

Privilege Escalation

Our last category of major database security issues is that of privilege escalation. In essence, privilege escalation is a category of attack in which we make use of any of a number of methods to increase the level of access above what we are authorized to have, or have managed to gain on the system or application through attack. Generally speaking, privilege escalation is aimed at gaining administrative access to the software in order to carry out other attacks without needing to worry about not having the access required.

As we mentioned earlier in the chapter, SQL injection is a very common attack against databases that are accessible through a Web interface and is largely an issue of not filtering or validating inputs properly. SQL injection can be used to gain information from the database in an unauthorized manner, modify data contained in the database, and perform many other similar activities. SQL injection can also be used to gain or escalate privileges in the database.

One of the more common SQL injection examples is to send the string ' or '1'='1 as the input in a username field for an application. If the application has not filtered the input properly, this may cause it to automatically record that we have entered a legitimate username, which we have clearly not done, allowing us to potentially escalate the level of privilege to which we have access.

ADDITIONAL RESOURCES

For those interested in more information regarding SQL injection and database security in general, two books available from Syngress are *Securing SQL Server* by Denny Cherry (ISBN: 9781597496254) and *SQL Injection Attacks and Defense* by Justin Clarke (ISBN: 9781597494243). Both are great resources from very knowledgeable folks.

An additional area of concern for privilege escalation is from an operating system perspective. Database applications are processes running on the operating system, using the credentials and privileges of an operating system user, just like a Web browser or any other application we might want to run. If we are not careful to protect our operating systems and the user accounts that run on them, as we talked about in Chapters 8 and 9, any database security measures we might put in place may be for naught. If an attacker gains access to the account under which the database software is running, he or she will likely have privileges to do anything he or she might care to do, including deleting the database itself, changing passwords for any of the database users, changing the settings for the way the database functions, manipulating data, and so on.

Our best defenses against operating system issues such as these are the set of hardening and mitigation steps we discussed in Chapter 9. If we can keep attackers from compromising our system in the first place, we can largely avoid this particular concern.

APPLICATION SECURITY TOOLS

We can use a number of tools in an attempt to assess and improve the security of our applications. We discussed some of them, such as sniffers, in Chapters 8 and 9. Others are less familiar and more complex, such as fuzzers and reverse engineering tools. Some of these tools require a certain amount of experience in developing software and a higher level of familiarity with the technologies concerned in order to be able to use them effectively.

Sniffers

As we discussed in Chapters 8 and 9, sniffers can be of great use in a variety of security situations. We can use them at a very high level to examine all the traffic traveling over the portion of the network to which we are attached, presuming we can get our sniffer placed properly to see the traffic in question. We can also use such tools very specifically in order to watch the network traffic being exchanged with a particular application or protocol. In Figure 10.3, we are using Wireshark to examine Hypertext Transfer Protocol (HTTP) traffic specifically.

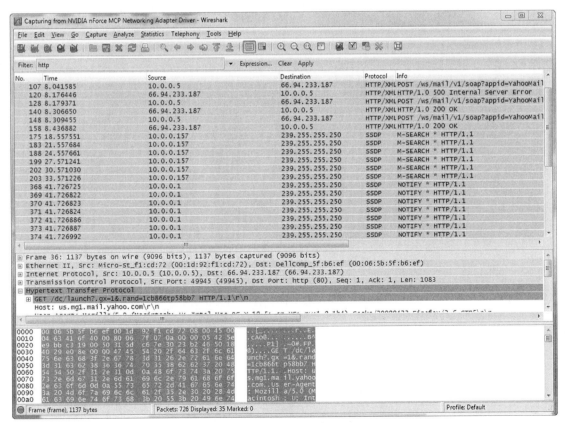

FIGURE 10.3
Wireshark Examining HTTP Traffic

We can also, in some cases, use tools specific to certain operating systems in order to get additional information from sniffing tools. A good example of this is the Microsoft Network Monitor tool, which will enable us to not only sniff the network traffic but also easily associate the traffic we are seeing with a particular application or process running on the system. This allows us to very specifically track information we see on the network interface of the system back to a certain process, as shown in Figure 10.4.

Web Application Analysis Tools

For purposes of analyzing Web pages or Web-based applications, a great number of tools exist, some of them commercial and some of them free. Most of these tools perform the same general set of tasks and will search for common flaws such as XSS or SQL injection flaws, as well as improperly set permissions, extraneous files, outdated software versions, and many more such items.

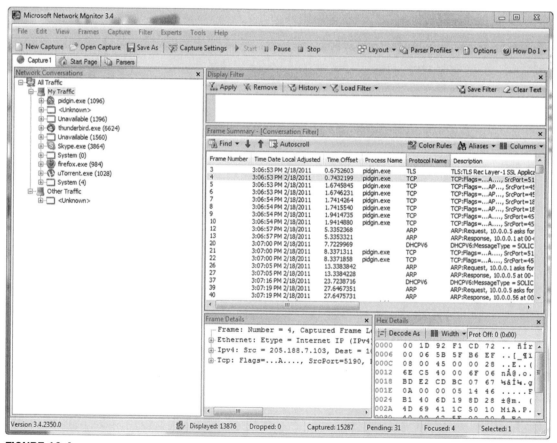

FIGURE 10.4
Microsoft Network Monitor Examining Traffic from an Application

NIKTO AND WIKTO

Nikto is a free and open source Web server analysis tool that will perform checks for many of the common vulnerabilities we mentioned at the beginning of this section and discussed earlier in the chapter when we went over server-side security issues. Nikto will index all the files and directories it can see on the target Web server, a process commonly referred to as spidering, and will then locate and report on any potential issues it finds.

> **ALERT!**
>
> It is important to note when using Web analysis tools that not everything the tool reports as a potential issue will actually be a security problem. Such tools almost universally give us back a certain number of false positives, indicating a problem that is not actually valid. It is important to manually verify that the issue really exists before taking action to mitigate it.

Nikto is a command-line interface tool that runs on Linux. For those of us who are in a Windows-centric environment, or prefer to use a graphical interface, SensePost has produced a Windows version of Nikto called Wikto, as shown in Figure 10.5. Wikto is very similar in functionality to Nikto and provides us with a GUI.

BURP SUITE

Quite a few commercial Web analysis tools are also available, and they vary in price from several hundred dollars to many thousands of dollars. Burp Suite is one such tool, tending toward the lower end of the cost scale for the professional version ($275 per year at the time of this writing) but still presenting a solid set of features. Burp Suite runs in a GUI interface, as shown in Figure 10.6, and, in addition to the standard set of features we might find in any Web assessment product, includes several more advanced tools for conducting more in-depth attacks.

Burp Suite is also available in a free version that allows the use of the standard scanning and assessment tools but does not include access to the more advanced features.

Fuzzers

In addition to all the tools we can use to look over our software for various known vulnerabilities, there is another category of tools we can use to find completely unexpected problems, a process referred to as fuzz testing. The tools we use for this technique, referred to as fuzzers, work by bombarding our applications with all manner of data and inputs from a wide variety of sources, in the hope that we can cause the application to fail or to perform in unexpected ways.

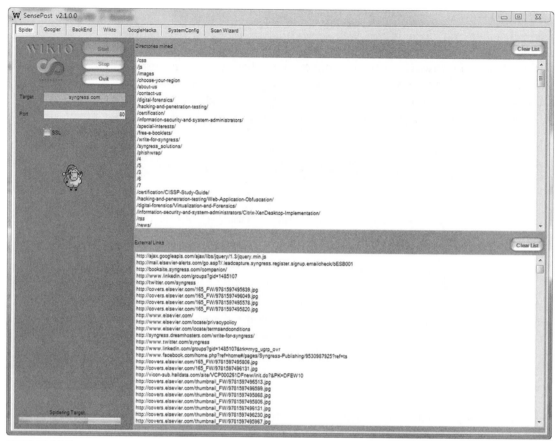

FIGURE 10.5
Wikto

> **MORE ADVANCED**
>
> The concept of fuzzing was first developed by Barton Miller for a graduate-level university operating system class in the late 1980s [9], and it has enjoyed popular use by security researchers and those conducting security assessments on applications. A great resource for further reading on fuzzing, including the document that spawned this field of analysis, can be found on Miller's fuzzing Web page at the University of Wisconsin, at http://pages.cs.wisc.edu/~bart/fuzz/.

A wide variety of fuzzing tools are available, some with a specific focus and some that are more general. Microsoft has released several very specific fuzzing tools to assist in discovering vulnerabilities in both existing software and software in development, including the MiniFuzz File Fuzzer, designed to find flaws in file-handling source code, the BinScope Binary Analyzer, for examining

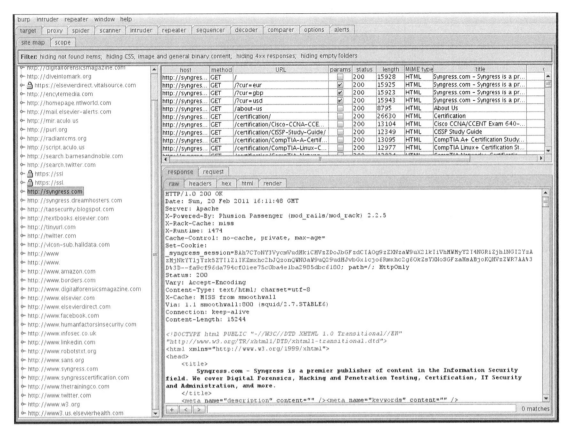

FIGURE 10.6
Burp Suite

source code for general good practices, and the SDL Regex Fuzzer, for testing certain pattern-matching expressions for potential vulnerabilities. A great number of other tools exist for a variety of fuzzing purposes, many of them free and open source.

APPLICATION SECURITY IN THE REAL WORLD

In today's highly networked and application-based business world, securing our applications is an absolute necessity. We work online, shop online, go to school online, conduct business online, and generally lead heavily connected lives. We can see frequent examples of businesses that do not take the trouble to secure their assets, and the serious repercussions that are felt by both them and their customers when they experience failure in this area.

We talked about the need to build security into our applications through the use of secure coding practices, the need to secure our Web applications, and the need to secure our databases, but these measures all really work in concert when we apply them. When we are developing an application, whether it is for use internally or whether it is Internet facing, we need to take all these areas into account. When we are developing an application from scratch, developing to a set of secure coding standards is an absolute must. The National Institute of Standards and Technology (NIST) 800 Series of publications[3] has numerous guides for both development and deployment of technologies and applications and is a great starting place for organizations that do not have internal development and deployment standards of their own.

Securing our Web applications and the databases they interface with is also a critical activity. When we look at any given breach that involved a lapse in security, whether corporate or governmental, we are almost guaranteed to find a failure in application security at some point. The TJX breach we discussed earlier in the chapter was not an application failure to begin with, but the lax application security the company had in place made the breach far worse than it might have been otherwise. Such security measures are not optional or just a "good idea" for technology-based companies, they are a foundational requirement. Depending on the industry in which we are operating and the data we are handling, such protections may be mandated by law.

[3] http://csrc.nist.gov/publications/PubsSPs.html.

SUMMARY

A number of vulnerabilities are common to the software development process, across many of the platforms on which we might be developing or implementing our solution. We may encounter buffer overflows, race conditions, input validation attacks, authentication attacks, authorization attacks, and cryptographic attacks, just to name a few. Although such issues are very common, most of them can be resolved with relative ease by following secure coding guidelines, either those internal to our organizations, or from external sources such as NIST, CERT, or the Build Security In Software Assurance Initiative (BSI) from the U.S. Department of Homeland Security.[4]

In terms of Web security, the areas of concern break out into client-side issues and server-side issues. Client-side issues involve attacks against the client software we are running, or the people using the software. We can help mitigate these by ensuring that we are on the most current version of the software and associated patches, and sometimes by adding extra security tools or plug-ins. On the other side, we have attacks that are directly against the Web server itself. Such attacks often take advantage of lack of strict permissions, lack of input validation, and leftover files from development or troubleshooting efforts. Fixing such issues requires careful scrutiny by both developers and security personnel.

Database security is a large concern for almost any Internet-facing application. The main categories of database security concerns are protocol issues, unauthenticated access, arbitrary code execution, and privilege escalation. Many of these problems can be mitigated by following secure coding practices, keeping

[4] https://buildsecurityin.us-cert.gov/bsi/home.html.

up-to-date on our software versions and patches, and following the principle of least privilege.

There are a number of application security tools that we can use in our efforts to render our applications more able to resist attack. As with network and host security, we can put sniffers to use in examining what enters and exits our applications in terms of network data. We can also use reverse engineering tools to examine how existing applications operate, and to determine what weaknesses we might have that a skilled reverse engineer could exploit. In addition, we can make use of fuzzing tools and Web application analysis tools in order to locate vulnerabilities, whether known or unknown.

EXERCISES

1. What does a fuzzing tool do?
2. Give an example of a race condition.
3. Why is it important to remove extraneous files from a Web server?
4. What does the tool Nikto do and in what situation might we use it?
5. Name the two main categories of Web security.
6. Is an SQL injection attack an attack on the database or an attack on the Web application?
7. Why is input validation important?
8. Explain a cross-site request forgery (XSRF) attack and what we might do to prevent it.
9. How might we use a sniffer to increase the security of our applications?
10. How can we prevent buffer overflows in our applications?

Bibliography

[1] J. Perira, How credit card data went out wireless door, Wall St. J. Online <http://online.wsj.com/article_email/article_print/SB117824446226991797->, 2007 (cited: February 14, 2011).

[2] A. Hickey, WEP: Wireless security's broken skeleton in the closet, SearchNetworking.com. <http://searchnetworking.techtarget.com/news/1252992/WEP-Wireless-securitys-broken-skeleton-in-the-closet>, April 26, 2007 (cited: February 14, 2011).

[3] P. Gregory, For an interesting account of the TJX breach, read their 10-K, Securitas Operandi, <http://peterhgregory.wordpress.com/2007/05/03/for-an-interesting-account-of-the-tjx-breach-read-their-10-k/>, May 3, 2007 (cited: February 14, 2011).

[4] M.L Sayao, Efficiency of Java and C# programming languages on Web applications or stand-alone projects, Associated Content. <www.associatedcontent.com/article/2947596/efficiency_of_java_and_c_programming.html>, May 30, 2010 (cited: March 9, 2010).

[5] I. Lucas, Password recovery speeds, Lockdown.co.uk. <www.lockdown.co.uk/?pg=combi>, July 10, 2009 (cited: November 20, 2010).

[6] L. Mearian, More flash drive firms warn of security flaw; NIST investigates, Computerworld. <www.computerworld.com/s/article/9143504/More_flash_drive_firms_warn_of_security_flaw_NIST_investigates?taxonomyId=17&pageNumber=1>, January 8, 2010 (cited: February 16, 2011).

[7] M. Deeg, S. Schreiber, Kryptografisch sicher? SySS knackt USB-Stick, SySS. <www.syss.de/fileadmin/ressources/040_veroeffentlichungen/dokumente/SySS_knackt_SanDisk_USB-Stick.pdf>, 2009.

[8] D. Litchfield, C. Anley, J. Heasman, B. Grindlay, The Database Hacker's Handbook: Defending Database Servers, Wiley, 2005. ISBN-13: 9780764578014.

[9] B. Miller, Fuzz Testing of Application Reliability, UW-Madison Computer Sciences. <http://pages.cs.wisc.edu/~bart/fuzz/>, May 25, 2008 (cited: February 19, 2011).

Index